# HAVE THE ATTITUDE!

## The Thinking That Makes
## Great Things Happen

CAROL QUINN

**Hire Authority, Inc.**
Delray Beach, Florida

*Have The Attitude!*
*The Thinking That Makes Great Things Happen*

Second Edition
ISBN # 0-9720872-2-2 (Soft cover)
ISBN # 0-9720872-3-0 (Hard cover)

**To order this book,
please call toll-free 1-866-638-0313**

*Editor with The Attitude:*
Diane Sears, DiVerse Media

*Cover Designer with The Attitude:*
Diane Trenary, Final Proof

*Layout/Page Designer with The Attitude:*
Michele DeFilippo, 1106 Design

*Photo Make-up Artist definitely with The Attitude:*
Grace Grenell

**Hire Authority, Inc.**
5884 Morningstar Circle, Suite 306
Delray Beach, FL 33484
(561) 638-0313

Published by HA Publishing. Printed in USA.

## ▼ ACKNOWLEDGING THOSE WITH THE ATTITUDE ▼

Extra special THANKS to Diane Sears, my fabulous editor and friend. Without you it wouldn't have been this good! For anyone who asks, you have my highest recommendations.

To Gene Quinn, thanks for rolling right along into the second book with me and providing me with unconditional support and assistance wherever and whenever I needed it.

To Jan Grenell, Dan Andrews, Jim Wilson, Tom Turner and Jane Persaud, thanks for playing with me. Each of you allowed me to test run the message to perfection. Your feedback and support was greatly appreciated.

I cannot forget about Maxine Jones and Daniel Scaduto for the contributions you each made as well as Steve Kirshenbaum for your daily inspirational quotes.

THANK YOU!

# ▼ TABLE OF CONTENTS ▼

## ▼ INTRODUCTION ▼

I wasn't even supposed to be there — it was just a total fluke. But there I was, getting out of my car at the mall shortly before noon on a weekday. I happened to look up into the sky, and at that very moment I witnessed the mid-air collision of two private airplanes. Four people died in that accident a few years ago. I had trouble stopping myself from thinking about what I had seen.

It was a few nights later when I had the dream. There was a group of people standing around an oval asphalt track. It looked like a track behind a high school where student athletes run, but this one was at a flight school and I was an instructor.

This particular flight school was different. It taught people how to fly without using an aircraft of any kind. The students were learning how to soar like birds. After some classroom instruction, everyone would go outside to this track. They would practice their takeoffs by running around the track until they reached a speed in which their feet would lift off the ground. It was so amazing and so profoundly inspirational to see.

As with any type of training, some people got the hang of it more quickly while others were slower to catch on — not that it really mattered either way. Some, however, became frustrated and wanted to quit, and still others thought it wasn't even possible to do in the first place. Hopelessness and discouragement quickly turned to amazement as people's feet actually lifted off the ground and they began to take flight. It was a phenomenal experience to witness these people's success!

There is a song about this very experience. It's performed by R. Kelly and is titled "I Believe I Can Fly." Here are some of the lyrics:

> I believe I can fly. I believe I can touch the sky.
> I think about it every night and day....
> I believe I can fly, if I just spread my wings.
> I believe I can soar,
> I see myself running through that open door.
> I believe I can fly because I believe in me!

You know, those four people who died in that plane crash were all pilots whose passion was flying. They lived their passion. One was a seasoned stunt pilot and the other three were Lear Jet pilots. So many of us never fulfill our dreams or accomplish our goals because we're focused on the possibility of "what if" a bad outcome were to happen.

Sure, sometimes bad things happen, and something bad happened that day. But so did something good. Those pilots never knew the lesson they had taught me. This lesson came from people I never even met. As horrible as the accident was, it showed me the brilliance of life. The chance that something bad may happen isn't enough to discourage high achievers. They take flight anyway in pursuit of their aspirations. These high fliers prefer to live life fully rather than sit on the sidelines and make excuses not to achieve.

You see, all high achievers have a common thread they share. It just happens to be their *attitude*. You've heard the sayings "*Attitude* is everything," "Hire the *attitude* and teach the skill" and "It's 90 percent *attitude* and 10 percent skill." This is *The Attitude* that everyone's talking about, the one that belongs to high achievers. And it's the reason these people are able to achieve more results and reign in the top 20 percent in job performance.

What exactly is their secret to success, you ask? Well, it's no longer a secret. It has been discovered. Do you wonder whether you share this common thread with them? Do you know whether you have *The Attitude*? Can you get it if you don't already have it? Is it something you can learn? Is it complicated? Absolutely, yes you can have *The Attitude* that high achievers have! You *can* learn what the high performers have already learned, and the answers are in the pages ahead.

Perhaps it wasn't a fluke that I was in that mall parking lot that day after all, because there began the vision for "Flight School." Its mission, to act as a catalyst to remove barriers and reveal every person's own unlimited potential to soar to great heights, became the purpose of this book. Perhaps the gift of inspiration that touched me so deeply as a result of the tragedy will expand to touch you, too. And so, Flight School begins...

## ▼ WHAT DOES THE FUTURE HOLD? ▼

W hat if you could identify high achievers just by looking at them? That might be nice, especially if you're
an employer conducting an interview. They would be the
ones wearing those dark sunglasses because their future is
so bright. OK, maybe that scenario is just the lyrics to a song,
but what a statement that would make. What an attitude it
would convey!

Seriously, do you ever notice that some people seem to
have an *attitude*? No, I mean the good kind? They have a positive attitude, and you just know great things are coming
their way. You always see them smiling. It's too bad the
future's not quite so bright for everyone else, though. I wonder how those people got to be selected? I want to be one of
the lucky ones. I want that *attitude*! I think we all do, in fact.
After all, this is what I have to look forward to today:

**HOROSCOPE —**
**Mental and emotional confusion**
**rule your day today.**
**Your best course of action**
**may be to fall silent.**

TODAY'S FORECAST —
Overcast, gloomy
with 80% chance of rain.
Might as well stay inside
and cancel any outdoor plans.

BUSINESS OUTLOOK —
The economy is in a recession
with no chance of a recovery on the horizon.
Better save your pennies.

Ever feel like you might as well go back to bed? Is it really as bleak as it appears to be sometimes? I mean, how can anyone really know for sure what the future holds for each one of us?

Is predicting the future left only to those people who have some kind of crystal ball, can read palms or have a direct connection to a higher power? I don't think so! History has had not only its share of "prophets of doom" but also those who have predicted greater things to come. Every day, if you look closely enough, *everyone* seems to be involved in some form of speculating or forecasting the future. We assess the odds of certain outcomes happening and adjust our actions accordingly. Whether we're predicting the weather, the stock market, or the response of another person, we respond according to what we *think* is going to happen.

The future — be it five years, five months, five days, five hours or five minutes from now — hasn't happened yet to anyone. What actually will happen is merely anyone's guess. "Sure things" have fallen through. The million-to-one odds of winning the lottery, well, they pay off to someone almost every week. And those things that "will never happen in a million years," those actually do happen. I wonder how people can be so absolutely sure how something will turn out. After all, they're just relying on speculation, right?

Thoughts regarding what's likely to happen vary among people. We know that. They may differ only slightly or they might differ dramatically, like night and day. Each person has the freedom to think whatever he or she wants to think. Our choices about what to think about or what viewpoint we take are virtually unlimited. We even have the power to change our minds and change our opinions at any time.

## ▼ WHERE GREAT ACCOMPLISHMENT STARTS ▼

If you were to create a list of man's greatest accomplishments, what would you include on this list? Would you include putting man on the moon, building a reusable spacecraft, or the invention of the airplane? How about the discovery of anesthesia, X-rays, smart pills or the cure for certain illnesses and diseases? What about the Stealth Bomber or smart bombs, microwave ovens, radios, televisions, telephones, or electricity? Then there are the pyramids in Egypt, the Great Wall of China and the Golden Gate Bridge, just to mention a few of the greatest architectural wonders of the world. Did you know that the Golden Gate Bridge was thought to be impossible to construct at one time? And that is true of everything on the list.

Before we landed a man on the moon, it was thought to be impossible. Before this project could begin, someone had to believe this monumental task could in fact be achieved. At least one person had to believe it was within reach. I am sure there were plenty of people who felt it was an impossible undertaking. They were the ones pointing out all the reasons why it couldn't be done or why it would never work. As the successes accumulated, I'm sure that's when more people got on board with the believers and finally realized the idea was not so far-fetched after all.

The one thing all great accomplishments have in common is that they started at some point with a single thought or idea. This thought was focused in the light of possibility — not in the darkness of inevitable defeat. Obstacles, failures, roadblocks and setbacks were all a part of changing the impossible to the possible...they always are. But for the optimistic thinker, there are no problems, only projects. Solutions are persistently sought until the desired outcome is achieved, thus deleting any problem.

## ▼ PROVING YOURSELF RIGHT ▼

Working diligently to find a way to make the impossible become possible would prove the negative, pessimistic thinkers wrong, and if you've ever noticed, people don't work too hard to prove that their own thinking is wrong. It's the people who believe something can be done who are working on a solution. They will even work overtime if that's what it takes. It's more than just coincidence — it's physiology. You just can't help it — you're wired to prove yourself right.

As part of our thinking process, we have a built-in device that is mechanically designed to always prove whatever we believe or think as being right or correct. This device is what links our behavior, our responses and our actions or lack of action to our thoughts. Our responses are not random or without rhyme or reason but rather directly linked to our thoughts and are in response to what we think and believe.

This built-in device that everyone has to prove oneself right works the same way whether you think you can achieve something or believe you cannot. It can work in your favor to help you achieve or it can hold you back from doing your best. It doesn't matter either way to this device. It just follows orders instead of questioning them. And it doesn't matter whether you are aware or unaware of how the thinking process works, either.

An easy distinction is to compare the higher achievers with those who achieve less. You see, the difference is that high achievers have figured out how to use the power of thought to their advantage. They have learned about the payoff that exists when you see things from a more optimistic point of view or as being possible to achieve, rather than impossible. This type of thinking pays off in their favor.

When Cesar Chavez was organizing the United Farm Workers of America, he challenged union members to say, "Si, se puede" when they didn't know how they would overcome obstacles. It means, "Yes, we can do it" or "Yes, it is possible." The farmworkers didn't think they could win without violence, but Chavez believed differently. Just as Hindu leader Mahatma Gandhi, Chavez believed a goal could be accomplished through persistence, hard work and faith. He believed the farmworkers could advance economic and social conditions through non-violent means, and that's exactly what they did.

Even if high achievers don't know how their goals will be realized, they believe and know it is possible even before they figure out how. They first conceive possibility, that it can be done, and then automatically follow these thoughts with ones focused on figuring out how. That's followed by the necessary action and effort until they achieve the goal, and it's all just an automatic process to prove their thinking right that is working in their favor. You get the thinking right and the action automatically follows. It's nothing magical. It's not even luck. It's just using the power of thought.

In essence, it's working in the exact same way for those who achieve less. From the start, they think a particular outcome is likely to be impossible. Since they are unable to conceive it, they can't see what they need to do in order to make it happen. Their thinking will naturally lead them to the appropriate response or behavior that matches their thoughts. But this time proving oneself right means putting less thought and less of one's self into the direction that will confirm that something *can* be done. Energy spent will be allocated toward going in the opposite direction — to prove it can't be done.

It's too bad the power of thought can be used as easily to sabotage a person's own success as it can to advance it. Whether you've heard this before or are hearing it for the first time, if you believed that *what you thought* never really mattered, this power brings quite an awakening. Now, all of a sudden, *what you think* becomes more important than you had previously imagined.

## ▼ THE WAY WE THINK ▼

In a recent interview with a magazine, I was asked about the different attitudes and how they show up differently in an interview with job applicants. The woman interviewing me for this article asked skeptically, "Do you mean to tell me that people really say they can't or couldn't do something regarding their job and then blame others for the reason why?" She added, "Wouldn't they know better than to say something like that?" I replied by telling her that's exactly what happens all the time and it's because people actually believe that there was nothing they could do, they believe what they are saying, and that's why they say it.

How we think and how we analyze information is a process we began learning early in childhood. The experts say a child's brain is 80 percent developed by age 5. Over time, this newly formed thinking process becomes established. By adulthood, it has become quite entrenched. A person gets so used to his or her way of thinking, it becomes a full-fledged habit. I call this "autopilot" thinking. As adults, we aren't even aware of the mechanics of our own thought process — we just keep on doing it the way we always have.

What's interesting about the thinking process is we are typically not aware of *how* we do it nor do we think of it as something we actually had to learn to do. Perhaps since we really cannot remember a time when we didn't know how to think, we believe thinking is innate and just assume we're doing it the best way. After all, no one thinks his or her own thinking is wrong or less effective.

We've never really stopped to consider that because thinking is a learned process, perhaps not all people are learning how to do it the same way. Or that one method of thinking can actually produce completely different results than another way of thinking, with some results being better than others. I don't believe most people have given much consideration to the idea that a person's way of thinking could be the real culprit that sabotages success — they think it's something else.

Even if you acknowledge that thinking varies, most people automatically assume that their learned way of thinking is the best and most-effective way of all. Most people are either not open to other ways of thinking or are so busy trying to keep up with their own fast-paced lives that they have never stopped long enough to evaluate the effectiveness of their own thinking process.

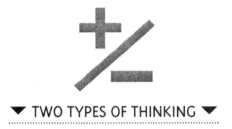

## ▼ TWO TYPES OF THINKING ▼

The more you have the opportunity to observe various job performance levels, the more you are able to see that a person's thinking process has the single greatest impact on what that person accomplishes. It ultimately explains why some people achieve more while others often struggle just to achieve very little.

How a person thinks about the future, what could or is likely to happen, falls into two groups or types of thought even though the thoughts themselves are infinite.

The first group is made up of those thoughts that are *active* in nature, meaning action-oriented. They are those thoughts that envision a positive or desirable outcome as one that is possible. It is called *active thought* because it is thinking that is focused on *how to accomplish the desired outcome,* and as a result it produces action intended to achieve the conceptualized outcome. Active thoughts are not only solution-oriented, they are genuinely optimistic, positive, hopeful and confident, supporting the belief that the best can happen. Active thoughts are part of the "I can" attitude, also known as *The Attitude.*

The second group, made up of passive thoughts, belongs to the prophets of doom. Passive thoughts predict future outcomes as being negative or contrary to the desired outcome.

They come from the belief that a specific outcome cannot be achieved and should be labeled as unrealistic. These thoughts are *passive* and discourage effort with their "Why bother to try? It'll never work and there is nothing I can do about it" thinking.

Negative thinking closes the mind off to a good outcome and shuts the door. As well as being passive, it's considered constricted or limited thinking, because it is blind to or eliminates viable options.

Positive thought focuses on possibility and expands the mind in search of a solution. It's not that an undesirable outcome cannot happen when you're thinking positive, solution-oriented thoughts. However, if that's what happens, you're still better equipped to find a solution than someone whose thinking restricts solutions.

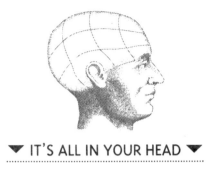

## ▼ IT'S ALL IN YOUR HEAD ▼

Have you ever wondered how possibility or impossibility is determined? I mean, there is no mechanical device or magical formula that computes this for us. All of the computing is done in our own mind. It's all simply a point of view, or you could even say it's an attitude. Once the mental calculations are done, the thought-processing mind determines how to best prove our assessment or prediction as being correct — whatever it may be.

"I can" thoughts or "It can be done" predictions put a person into action, whereas "I can't" thinking doesn't. If a person truly believes an outcome can be accomplished, then the equivalent actions are dispensed to assist in proving this to be right. Thinking that is determined to accomplish produces a positive or active response — unlike the response from "it can't be done" thinking, which produces the opposite type, one that is negative or is passive. *How you respond and what you are willing to do is dependent upon what you predict the outcome is most likely to be.* The more you think a specific outcome is possible and the more convinced you are of this, the more YOU are willing to DO to make this outcome a reality. This type of thinker will move heaven and earth to make it so, and this type of thinker will produce more results.

Conversely, the less you are convinced an outcome is likely to happen, then the less effort you are willing to expend toward trying to achieve something you don't believe to be possible. *This mental process of envisioning the future ultimately determines the effort that we will expend to make a specific outcome happen.* The more we believe, the more we try and also the more we keep trying. The less we believe, the less effort we expend and the more we will be prone to giving up easily.

This entire thinking process is constantly taking place without us ever being aware of it. The power of the mind is amazing when you think about it! It operates in split-second time in whichever method we learned. So we often don't credit our thoughts as being the reason behind our actions. And if we were more aware of the thoughts we think and the power they have, we'd realize that changing our thinking could have a dramatic impact on our life. Even though thought happens in an instant, if you were to take the time to investigate more closely, you'd actually be able to see how you operate.

I saw this at work in myself some time ago while I was at the beach. I had helped a couple who parked nearby carry their beach items down to the sand. We sat near each other, and the wife asked whether I was single, available and interested in meeting a nice man they were expecting to join them. I was single. However, prior to answering her, what flashed in my head was a not-so-pretty picture of what someone else might consider nice. With this thought in mind, I decided to save myself some trouble. I said no.

As it turned out, the man the couple had in mind for me was someone I definitely would have been interested in meeting. He looked like a nice, clean-cut professional in my age bracket.

Needless to say, I was a bit frustrated with myself for the answer I had chosen. My negative thoughts had prevented me from meeting him.

As the old saying goes, "Nothing ventured, nothing gained," and I had gained nothing because of my own thinking. We close doors, reject opportunities and reduce our chances of achieving the outcome we desire, usually without realizing that our own thinking is the culprit. Our responses are connected to the split-second thinking process going on in our heads all the time.

▼ PLACEBO EFFECT — IF YOU REALLY BELIEVED... ▼

Here's a question for you to ponder. If it's really true and you believed your thoughts had the power to determine or at least affect what happened, would you choose different thoughts? It makes you stop and wonder about how responsibly or effectively we are all thinking.

The power of thought is often underestimated. Take, for example, *placebo*, which means, "I will please." The power of the placebo effect has been known in the medical and research communities for a long time. This is how it works: To test the effectiveness of a new drug, participants in a study group are given either the actual drug or a placebo, a pill that looks exactly the same as the drug but is made of sugar. Unable to tell the difference, participants do not know which they are receiving.

A 1959 study showed that the placebo was 70 percent as effective as morphine for controlling pain. The placebo's power comes from the patient's expectation rather than the pill's chemical make-up.

Placebos have a tremendous psychological impact, but that by no means suggests that the patient's pain is all in the head. It's not saying the discomfort is not real. To the contrary. According to an article in *USA Today* titled "Take one. You'll feel better," hundreds of scientists at the National Institutes of Health in Bethesda, Md., discussed what was known and not known about the placebo effect. They not only discussed the scientific research data, they spoke of the healing power of hope and expectation. Patients who focused on or believed there was a chance they would feel better and recover responded favorably even in the absence of the drug or placebo.

Scientists speculate that a placebo works by stimulating endorphins in the brain. Ethicist Howard Brody, a family practitioner at Michigan State University, says, "You don't need the sugar pill to unleash these important forces." The placebo effect suggests that cures do not just come from pill bottles or high-tech equipment or procedures, that engaging the power of the mind to aid in the healing process has greater potential than we have yet discovered.

It seems that thinking good thoughts not only feels good, it's also good for us. Some researchers have gone as far as to suggest that pessimism may be harmful to your health by boosting levels of destructive stress hormones in your bloodstream. No one completely understands how a positive attitude helps people recover more quickly, but mounting evidence suggests it has something to do with the mind's power.

A study in the 1960s gave 12 psychology graduate students several rats to train. Half of the students were told they were working with genetically bred rats that were very smart and would learn quickly. The other half were told their rats were genetically bred to be slow learners. At the end of the experiment, it was determined that the "smart" rats did, indeed, learn exceptionally well and that the "stupid" rats did, in fact, do poorly.

However, there is one catch. What the students did not know is that there was no difference between the rats. The rodents were all the same. None of them had been genetically altered.

Similar experiments have been conducted with schoolchildren and their teachers, and also at the U.S. Air Force Academy with enlisted airmen, all of which produced the same kinds of results. Some teachers were told they had a group of slow learners and others were told they were teaching gifted students. All of the students, however, were similar in their learning ability — yet the results were equivalent to what the teachers believed.

The power of your beliefs or expectations does have an effect on what happens. What you think an outcome will be in advance of it happening does affect your results. Changing your prediction, changing what you think, could in fact make all the difference in the world in the results you achieve.

Comedian Bill Cosby, being interviewed on *Good Morning America* by Diane Sawyer, spoke of a time early in his career when he absolutely bombed on stage. He said he was so terrible, it was a turning point in his career. He seriously thought about quitting the business. He went on to say that he had done all of this to himself. He recalled that before he went onto stage that night, he had become so worked up that he had convinced himself he wasn't a very good comedian. He said what he actually did out there in front of the audience that night was prove his own thinking right.

Afterward, offstage, the club manager even went to Cosby and said the comedian who had just performed, whoever he was, stunk. He said he knew, however, that Bill Cosby was great. Cosby re-thought things and went back out for his second set, and it went great that time. Just think: This high achiever had almost talked himself into quitting. I wonder how many others actually do quit before their great talents have the opportunity to take flight. I'm sure glad Bill Cosby didn't quit, because I've always enjoyed him as a comedian.

In the study involving the rats, the students who believed they had superior rats treated their rats differently than those students who thought their rats wouldn't learn no matter what they did. It was out of their control, *or so they thought.* Instead of handling their rats gently, giving them attention and coaxing them with treats, as the students with the "smart" rats did, the students who thought they had unintelligent rats handled them very sparingly — and when they did, they only picked them up by their tails. What they thought did affect their actions, which did have a powerful impact on what ultimately happened. *Simply a change in thinking could have produced a different set of results for those who believed there was nothing they could do.*

## ▼ WHAT CHOICE DID I REALLY HAVE? ▼

Comprehending that you have choices and control over what you think is the foundation for more effective thinking. It's the secret to high achievement.

Unfortunately, many of us grew up without learning about the power or how to operate it in a way that serves us well. If we never learn to manage our thoughts, our thoughts are allowed to run randomly and manage us instead. It's not something that happens on purpose. It's more like a child never learning appropriate and inappropriate behaviors, and being allowed to run out of control without any discipline. Being problem-focused comes from not knowing any better and allowing our thoughts to run without being reeled in. We are all byproducts of our own thinking even when we allow unmanaged thoughts to manage us. There is always a consequence.

I remember a fictional story of a man trapped in a cellar for many years. This man would scream out, "Let me out! Let me out!" He would shout for help, but no one ever came to his rescue. He would kick and beat on the door, but it never opened. One day he became so fed up with his situation that he decided once and for all to find a way to get out. He went to the door and began jiggling the doorknob, and amazingly the door sprang open. To his surprise, he discovered the door had never been locked. In fact, it had no lock at all. The man had assumed he was trapped against his will when he was the one who had held the key to his freedom all along but never realized it.

At any given time, we have much more control than we recognize or accept. Think about it. Every day, in every moment, we have control over our many choices. We can speak up kindly or harshly, or we can say nothing at all. We can ask for assistance or assume no one will help. We can choose to accept what we don't want or do something to change it. We can walk away or we can keep trying.

We can say we have no alternative or we can see more options. We can think happy thoughts or sad ones instead. We can see a person's good or we can focus only on flaws. We can see the most hopeful outcome or can dwell on the worst. We can get stuck in the past or see the best that's yet to come. We can find things to be grateful for or choose resentment for what we lack.

When we get knocked down, we can get back up or we can stay down. We can help ourselves or wait to be helped. We can even turn help down when it shows up. We can give in or give of ourselves. We can look for solutions and ways to make things better or choose to believe solutions do not exist.

Choices, choices, choices. We all have them, even if we deny it. At any time, we can even choose a different option than we chose in the past. Yet, too often I hear people say, "I had no choice," "My hands were tied" or "There was nothing I could do." Know the difference between not liking an option and not having an option.

Here's an example. Let's say you hate your present job. You have some options here. You can wait for the boss to see things differently and to change because the boss, after all, is the problem. You can be negative and bad-mouth your boss and the company and overall express how miserable you are on the job. You can act disinterested and do only the minimum amount of work you can get away with and be a low-performing employee. You can voice how unfair you think things are and explain all the flaws you've found to anyone who will listen.

You can choose one or more of these above options, all of which probably will make you look bad, even though we don't always see it that way.

Now, there are also more choices, ones that would benefit you more. You could put on a happy face. You may try looking for a different position within the same company, or take on tasks that would make you more marketable for your next job. You could perform your job well and project a positive attitude, which instead would enhance your professional reputation. You could keep your negativity to yourself and say nothing when you can't say anything good, all at the same time you are hunting for a new job.

See the positive, say something nice, smile, show interest, go the extra mile, find a solution. Or add to the problem, show frustration and anger, be negative, become indifferent, make things more difficult. All of these are choices, and they are under your control. Discarding them, discrediting them, not considering them or not recognizing them does not change the fact that they are still viable options available to you.

Make a change in your thinking in either direction, from pessimistic to positive or from positive to negative, and watch how the world responds to you differently than before. Perhaps you have more control under your power than you actually realized.

Comprehending that you have some control in your life and in what happens seems to be good for you. People who don't believe they have control over their own lives develop a sense of passivity and helplessness, according to Bernie Siegel, a physician, speaker and best-selling author known for encouraging people to tap into their own healing power to overcome adversity.

Evidence shows that your attitude about life can improve your health and even speed your recovery time from a serious illness, surgery or loss. "The attitude that seems to help the most is optimism, hope and, above all, a feeling that you have some control over or can have an impact on the quality of your own life," says Suzanne Segerstrom, Ph.D, a University of Kentucky Psychology Department assistant professor who has studied the effects of optimism on a person's health.

Understanding the impact that perception of control, or the lack of it, has on a person's life has its own specialized area of study within psychology called locus of control. According to psychologist Hebert Lefcourt, in his book titled *Locus of Control*, "Whether people believe that they can determine their own fate, within limits, is of critical importance to the way in which they engage in challenges." Control boils down to how much power a person believes he or she has to produce intended results by conquering the obstacles that block the way.

The word *locus* means location, place or source. Locus of control is *where* power or control is *thought* to reside — in other words, who or what has the power or control and gets to determine an outcome. It is either believed to be internal, meaning the power is within oneself, or it is not, in which case control over an outcome is seen as being external of oneself.

An external source could be anyone or anything other than oneself — who or what isn't important. It doesn't matter whether the external controller is specifically identified, such as "the boss," or it's more ambiguous, such as "they" or bad luck, destiny or fate.

When we talk about our control, *what* we think we *can and can't* control varies among people. For example, most of us would agree that we cannot control the weather, so we don't even try. But not 100 percent will agree with this. Some people believe that we do have some control over our weather and we could have more if we figured out how. For example, Native Americans have long used rain dance rituals to cause precipitation, and modern researchers have studied ways to alter weather through the science of cloud seeding.

What one person believes is impossible, another person thinks is attainable. It goes back to the beginning of the book about our prediction of an outcome. You see, in order to give ourselves the go-ahead to try, we must think that it's possible to achieve before we'll expend the necessary effort to make it happen. There may be nothing more powerful than a made-up mind.

This makes locus of control tied to motivation. Internal perceived control, also known as internal motivation, is when you see yourself as possessing the power to affect an outcome or, more specifically, to achieve a desired outcome. You are the driver, you put yourself into motion and you know you're able to steer yourself to your desired outcome and *will* eventually get there just as long as you don't quit first. You are self-motivated.

External control, on the other hand, means one sees oneself as being powerless to affect or determine an outcome. People who do not believe in their own power see the external world as being in charge of what happens. These people see themselves as only being along for the ride, like passengers who have very little say.

Perception of control is a learned thought process, and the difference between an internal and external perception of control is just a variance in thinking, that's all. The viewpoint that the external world is in charge and that there is nothing a person can do about it is a misconception, which is the result of learned thinking that distorts reality, making it not very effective.

All people have more control to affect what happens than they actually realize. The key is to become aware of the thoughts that see oneself as lacking power and then replace them with truer thoughts, ones that recognize one's greatest potential. It sounds so simple, doesn't it? Achievement is more accessible than we perhaps realized if we'd just stop blocking our potential. The high performer believes in himself and believes he can achieve, and this is what gives rise to his higher level of accomplishment.

The power of thought has inspired many. Just listen to music. The words to countless songs refer to this amazing power. For example, in the duet by Mariah Carey and Whitney Houston "When You Believe," the lyrics read: *Who knows what miracles you can achieve when you believe somehow you will. You will when you believe.*

When perceived control is not recognized or believed, it's thought to not even exist at all. The person's negative thinking causes personal sabotage because it conceals the truth about that person's actual potential. It renders the person powerless in his or her own eyes, all because of that person's thoughts. It's not something that's being done to that person by the external world.

A person with the "I can" optimistic attitude recognizes his own power, whereas someone with an "I can't" attitude has not yet made this connection. The words "I can't" are words that clearly deny a person's power to produce results. "I can't" thinking is de-motivating. It's thinking that takes the wind out of a person's sails.

Listen: "I can't. I can't do that. It's not under my control. I'm not able. It can't be done!" The "I can't" thinker perceives himself as having little to no personal control over what happens, so the power must belong elsewhere, somewhere external of him. This is an underassessment of one's own power, not an accurate determination of one's actual power.

It's simple. *In any situation or experience in which you see the outside world as having more power and control than you do, and you see yourself as being helpless to do anything, you are not seeing your full potential and have relinquished some or all of your own power.*

## ▼ THE SENSE-OF-SELF SCALE ▼

How developed or under-developed your perception of control is makes all the difference in the world regarding how you view the obstacles and adversity that block your path. Let's use the analogy of a balance scale to explain how perceived control is viewed differently between internally and externally motivated people. This particular type of scale has a T-shaped frame and two pans, one connected to each side. It is used to compare the weight of two different items when one is placed in each pan.

Imagine that we place our "sense of self" on the left pan. Sense of self refers to the amount of control we see ourselves having to conquer obstacles and achieve a desired outcome. On the other side of the scale, let's place whatever blocks our path to any desired outcome. In this pan are adversity, obstacles, difficult people, problems, unfortunate circumstances, whatever roadblocks you are up against.

This scale does not measure in pounds and ounces like most scales. Instead, it compares the two sides to each other to determine which weighs more. This particular scale uses our own judgment or perception to assess what each side is believed to weigh.

Here is how it works: The side believed to weigh the most has control and power over an outcome. Only the left side of the scale, which contains the beliefs we have about ourselves, is what truly interests us. It is this side that will ultimately determine who or what has control, also known as our perceived control. I'll explain why.

If the person making this assessment does not realize his own power, meaning he underestimates himself and what he can do, the obstacle or adversity will almost always appear to weigh more than his side of the scale does. When a person underestimates his own power to affect results, then everything is skewed. Both sides of the scale are viewed incorrectly. When "self" is seen as smaller than it really is, from that vantage point the rest of the world looks much larger than it is in actuality. It could be compared to a child's view of the world, where adults all appear to be giant.

This process of underestimating oneself is actually common — it's almost like an epidemic, sadly enough. Whenever it's happening, a person sees himself as having the lesser power, thus being the one *not* in control and ultimately not someone who can influence results. When control is perceived to be external of oneself instead of internal, expending effort is often seen as futile.

The actual size of the difficulty on the right side of the scale is not what matters, it's a person's own sense of self that is the important measurement. A strong sense of self knows it can conquer anything without regard to size. Not only does a healthy sense of self view an obstacle in correct proportions in relationship to oneself, the obstacle is not seen as having the greater power and therefore is not something that can determine an outcome for a person who knows he can achieve. Perception is powerful — especially the perception one has of oneself.

Eighteenth century French philosopher Voltaire wrote that "love of ourselves is the basis of all our opinions and all our actions." A person with a low, underdeveloped self-esteem doesn't quite believe he can overcome the adversity he encounters and isn't able to muster the necessary mental power to do so, and therefore this individual doesn't try. This person often takes the path of least resistance — which, by the way, is *not* the path of conquering the obstacle. This person goes in a different direction instead.

I remember this homeless man I met. It was during a time when the economy was booming and employers were begging to fill their job openings, especially those lower-paying, no-skills-required jobs. With the existence of support groups that help the downtrodden get back on their feet, I couldn't understand why this man was choosing to be a homeless panhandler rather than be employed, so I asked him. He responded by saying he couldn't get a job because he wasn't good enough. The life he was living was equivalent to his thinking about himself.

The homeless man is an example of an extreme case. However, when "self" is seen as powerless to defeat those obstacles that appear to be gigantic, the person really has no alternative than to give up. Might as well save one's breath and energy, and hope for the best. Seeing the problem as being larger than oneself is not an issue of having a problem that is insurmountable or impossible to conquer. It is the person's thinking that creates defeat because it limits solutions, blocks ideas and shoots down viable options, all to prove the obstacle was truly unconquerable.

For people who are problem-focused, the actual solving of their current problems will not get them out of being in problems. They will continuously get stuck in them because their learned thinking process, which is now a habit, did not include correctly viewing and dealing with the problems they encounter. They never learned how to effectively overcome obstacles. Their problems of the present may eventually move on, but their thinking continues to be the same, so the cycle repeats.

This mental comparison process that occurs on the T-scale is always going on, but it's usually without our awareness of it. Depending on how much we acknowledge or deny our own power, we will either encourage or discourage ourselves.

I've always liked a story Joan Lunden, television host for "Good Morning America" for 15 years, told during an interview. She said when she was growing up, her father never allowed her to say "I can't." He would tell her there was nothing she could not do if she made up her mind. So many people have learned the power of "I can't," however, that they have not yet learned about the power that comes with saying "I can do this!" Lunden did, and she achieved unprecedented success in an industry that previously spotlighted few women.

## ▼ ACHIEVEMENT BEGINS IN THE MIND ▼

You may think your attitude is a reflection of your life, but it's not. It's the other way around. Your life is really a reflection of your attitude. What you think creates your world. What you think does have an impact, and its greatest repercussions are on you, the one thinking the thoughts.

You see, achievement and the lack of it both start in the mind. It's exactly as American automobile magnate Henry Ford said, "Whether you think you can or you cannot, you're right." You are what you think you are. Whether you think "I can" thoughts or "I can't do it" thoughts really does make all the difference when it comes to achievement. You and only you have the choice of how you envision an outcome, where you place your focus, and whether you can or cannot, all of which will have a direct impact on your life by determining your actions that follow.

To *conceive* means to form in the mind. U.S. astronaut Edgar Mitchell, the lunar module pilot aboard the Apollo 14 mission to the moon in 1971, said it boldly: "Mass is merely dense thought." Where you place your focus is what you create. The invention of the telephone, for example, started out as an idea. It eventually grew from thought form into mass form, or physical form.

It is like the making of a movie. What you think is what is "Now Showing" on your mental movie screen, and it's going to unfold in front of your very eyes. Your actions make you the lead actor playing out the script that you've envisioned with your own thoughts. And only by changing your thoughts can you change the script and change the role you personally play, which will cause the outcome of the movie to change. Realize it or not, you are both the actor and the director of the movie starring you. It is your thinking that is being acted out.

As the star in your own movie, you should know the tremendous influence of "I can." It shouts "ACTION!" It says, *"I have the power! I can prevail over the obstacle!"* It proclaims that you have the power instead of lacking it.

TV talk show host and best-selling author Iyanla Vanzant, in her book *Until Today,* states:

**It is arrogant of you to assume that you are incapable because you don't believe you are capable.
You have gifts. You have the gift of intellect.
You can think yourself into and out of any situation with which you are confronted. You have the ability to speak for yourself. You can defend yourself!
That is power. You are powerful! Now, why don't you try acting like it? Just for today, know that you are powerful. Embrace your power! Start by being grateful for the power you have been given and are using free of charge! Today I am devoted to experiencing myself as a powerful being!**

U.S. President Harry Truman once said, "A pessimist is one who makes difficulties of his opportunities, and an optimist is one who makes opportunities of his difficulties." The difference is in how different people see similar circumstances. Some will turn their lemons into lemonade and their stumbling blocks into steppingstones, while others won't.

To quote Rick Pitino, the coach who led the Kentucky Wildcats college basketball team to a national championship in 1996, "Success is a choice." High achievers are ordinary people who produce more results because they have figured out how to use the power of *The Attitude* so it works to their advantage.

## ▼ 90,000 UNITS OF ENERGY PER DAY ▼

Here is another way to look at thought that may help you to better understand its power and how it works. The mind is a very busy place. We think approximately 90,000 thoughts per day. However, you can think only one thought at a time. You can switch from one to another instantly but still have only one at time. While you are thinking one particular thought, such as "I can't," you cannot also think about finding a solution or think in the terms of possibility. You cannot believe that you both lack power and possess it at the same time regarding the same issue.

Inventory what you spend most of your time thinking about in each area of your life. Do you focus 50 percent or more of your thoughts on how bad things are, on the "if only's," and on how you've been wronged or are stuck? Or do you spend more time thinking about what you can do to reach your goals, find a solution or do something better? Either way of thinking is a learned habit.

It is our predominant thought that will determine our behavior, response or action. When someone's "attitude is showing," it's really his or her habit of thinking that is exposed. The greatest impact of your thoughts will be on you, not on someone else. When you finally realize this, it will all of a sudden shed new light on the importance of choosing your thoughts wisely.

Think of each thought as being one unit of energy with each day having 90,000 units of energy available. The focus of your thoughts becomes the focus of your energy. The greater your focus, the greater the energy you give to shaping that type of outcome. Imagine what you could achieve with a mind full of "I can" thought energy. Think of the high achiever as someone who spends most of his time figuring out solutions for those things he doesn't know how to do...yet.

Perhaps it's better stated to say 90,000 units of pure *power* instead. What we often do, however, is make the mistake of giving some of our thought to the desired outcome but then giving more thought to how it probably won't happen. Or we get into trouble with thinking that only selected thoughts of ours have power and the rest do not. It doesn't work that way. We are using our power to prove that we can't or prove that we can, or we're diluting it by mixing it between both beliefs. We reduce our power to produce results when we don't use all of the power that we have available to us because we never learned how.

A friend of mine with a brother who is a very successful businessman says the brother grew up never learning that he couldn't. The problem isn't ever that something is impossible. It's *thinking* something can't be done, it's the *thinking* that contradicts possibility that is the problem. The thoughts we focus on the most have the single greatest impact on our life. What you choose to think about determines where you are directing your power.

In the movie *Back to the Future*, which is about time travel, an optimistic character named George McFly says, "If you put your mind to it, you can accomplish anything!" Unfortunately, there are many times when we don't make up our minds that we can achieve, so we never fully unleash the power we possess, at least not as much as we could.

Another famous optimist of film, Master Yoda from *Star Wars*, had *The Attitude*. He said, "Try not. Do or do not do!" That quote is about making up your mind to do something or choosing not to do it, but not doing something halfheartedly in between. It's about either finding a way to achieve or not even trying — "Try not." To say you'll *try* means you'll expend some effort and maybe you'll do what it takes to achieve results and maybe you won't. It's a mind that is not fully convinced and cannot conceive the desired outcome, which means it is not operating in its full power.

There are many who inadvertently misuse their power because they don't know they have it or know how to use it effectively. Some people choose to reject their power so they don't have to take responsibility for it. Denial or rejection does not change the existence of it, however. The power does exist.

It is not about whether we possess it or not. It's absolutely not about being one of the chosen few who have been given this power. It's about our own recognition and effective use of the power that everyone already has. We can do anything we make up our mind to do, but first we must make up our own mind. What really distinguishes people from each other is less about their physical differences or their varied personal circumstances but rather the way they think. *Attitude really is everything!*

## ▼ NEGATIVE "KRYPTONITE" THOUGHTS ▼

The word or label of "negative" refers to something that's not good. Because of its connotation, if people with negative thoughts were to recognize their own negativity, they probably would stop it. But the reality is, it's actually easier and much safer to recognize this in someone else, so we often don't see it in ourselves. Most people will automatically place themselves into the category of being positive thinkers even when they are not.

Webster's dictionary defines the word negative as *opposed to the positive, containing negation, having lower potential or being without reward or result, expressing resistance, to lack constructiveness or helpfulness, arguing against a resolution, to disprove, deny or refute.*

Negative thoughts and comments are not acknowledged as being negative even though they really are. People do not fully recognize the extent of their own negative thinking because they deem negativity to be something different than what it really is. "It's something someone else does, not me. None of my thoughts or comments lacks constructiveness, denies possibility, or reduces potential results."

The truth is, whether we're positive people or not, we *all* get caught up in constricted thinking that disputes the possibility of a certain outcome happening rather than focusing on finding a way. Aware of it or not, it's something that we *all* do. Believing that you are never negative is more of a problem than recognizing the fact that you do think negative thoughts.

In my book *Don't Hire Anyone Without Me*, negative thoughts are compared to Kryptonite, a fictional substance that depletes Superman's energy and drains his power. Some people carry around this stuff, usually without ever knowing. They're zapped of their energy, and instead of being able to perform to their fullest, they become merely average-performing mortals. Imagine everyone having the power to be just like Superman, to do remarkable work and soar to great heights if they'd simply lose the Kryptonite that is attached to their negative attitude.

It's the people who spend time thinking about how to achieve their desired results, who view it as being possible instead of impossible, who achieve the most results. French writer and philosopher Voltaire said, "No problem can withstand the assault of sustained thinking." That's only partially true, however. It's not just ANY sustained thinking, it's the assault of relentlessly focusing on how to solve the problem. It's thinking that it CAN be solved — not the sustained thinking that it's hopeless.

Negative thinking does more damage than just deny possibility. It contains thoughts that relinquish a person's sense of control. These thoughts are not an accurate representation of reality, despite the fact they may appear to be to the person thinking them. Unaware that pessimism is merely a perception or point of view that is a learned habit, most negative people are completely ignorant of what their own thinking is doing to them. Not trying, giving up, being negative and being problem-focused are all just byproducts of our own thinking that lacks the perception of personal control.

You've heard the saying "Perception is reality." Well, many people don't see how they are contributing to the results they achieve, whether they get the desired outcome or not. It's like they're saying, "I am on this earth as a human being, and everything I do, say and think has absolutely ZERO effect on everyone and everything around me."

Or perhaps it's more along the lines of "selective existence" — "I can have an impact, but it's only on those things I choose to affect." It is similar to the thinking that only some selected thoughts have power, but not all of them do. We are wasting a lot of our potential by using only part of our power. Since we know control is a point of view and it varies among people, perhaps our own perception of control is one that is skewed or limited by negative thoughts that we're not even aware exist. It's when a person realizes how his or her own thinking is actually less effective than it could be that the person can begin to turn things around.

Even though none of us typically receives formal childhood training on how to think, it doesn't mean we don't learn. Formally or informally, somewhere and somehow along the way we all learned to think the way we do today. But the truth is, all of us have grown up learning less than purely positive thinking — yes, every single one of us, including me. I'm considered a very positive person, and I'm surprised just how often I catch my own subtle and not-so-subtle thoughts that are saboteurs of my own success.

Without personal awareness and openness, people believe they already possess 100 percent perfect thinking. If that's the case, then there is no room for improvement. After all, you cannot improve upon perfection.

It doesn't matter where you've been, what you've done, who you are, how old you are, or what's been done to you and why. It doesn't even matter how you've always done it.

What matters right now is what you do from this point forward. It's about learning the mechanics of thought and how to use the power of thought more effectively with the ultimate goal of producing better results for yourself — that is, if you desire.

Starting right now, all of us can learn to think more effectively than we have before, and that includes me.

## ▼ NEW MOTIVATION ▼

You should understand by now, at least in concept, that "I can't" and "It can't be done" thinking is not about something being unachievable in real life but instead the result of ineffective thinking. The issue is, it's about something that's mentally inconceivable, not something that's actually impossible. When we cannot conceive, we don't believe.

We know this type of thinking works mostly on proving that which we'd rather *not* have happen. We must address our own ability to conceptualize our desired outcomes. Put to music in the 1996 popular song "I Believe I Can Fly" by R. Kelly, the concept is explained this way: *I use to think that I could not go on, and life was nothing but an awful song, you see, I was on the verge of breaking down. There are miracles in life I must achieve, but first I know it starts inside of me. If I can see it, then I can do it. If I just believe it, there's nothing to it. I believe I can fly!* Just imagine what could be done if we simply adopted an optimistic way of thinking and believed more in happy outcomes.

Often I use the term "New Motivation" to describe this increase in producing desired results that comes from a positive change in attitude. And please don't call me a motivational speaker or writer. I technically cannot motivate you or anyone else — only *you* can motivate you. "New Motivation" is an oxymoron. First of all, it's not new at all but it is to so many people. And secondly, it truly is the ONLY motivation there is…it's the real McCoy.

Yes, there are external motivators that do get people moving, but they are merely artificial imitators of motivation that are only temporary. When you talk about motivating another person, that makes you an external motivator. Sure, you can encourage a person to take action or to get moving, but don't expect it to last without your continued prodding. As soon as the external motivator is out of sight, then it's also out of mind.

It wasn't real in the first place because it didn't genuinely belong to the person being motivated. Therefore, I don't believe you can really consider it motivation at all. It's more of a fire that's being lit under someone. The fire is the motivation, but it doesn't exist on the inside of that person, it's only external. When the fire is hot, it works fairly well to put the person it's intended for into action. But when it goes out, action, effort and persistence fizzle out, too.

True motivation is a flame that burns internally, and it stays lit even when the going gets tough. For this fire, difficult conditions such as wind or drought can make it blaze stronger than ever. Adversity does not cause the fire to go out, nor does it force people to quit. True motivation is what keeps people going even when they're discouraged because the "I can do it" is genuinely believed. This internal fire is actually protected from outer conditions. It's the fire that's still burning inside that pushes a person onward, motivating that person to continue, refusing to let that person quit.

True motivation is sustained. It's perseverance. It is a willingness to do what it takes to produce the desired outcome. That includes hurdling the obstacles and turning a deaf ear to naysayers. It's getting back up every time you fall and, if necessary, getting up again and again and again.

Motivation really is about the drive that boils up from somewhere inside like an endless spring. Most importantly, true motivation is not dependent on other people or things to keep it going. The key to motivation is its power source — motivation is thought-powered. Everyone has it, and we are all either using it to our advantage or not. It all begins within, with our thoughts.

Motivation, motivational speakers, motivational books and messages are merely external hype that will quickly wear off unless you are able to see the power that resides within you and, in fact, resides in everyone. Internal or self-motivation happens *only* when people realize the power they possess within themselves and stop thinking "I can't."

## ▼ SHIFTING POWER ▼

**B**oth high achievers and those who achieve less encounter obstacles. Neither group knows how to conquer these roadblocks initially. And yes, some obstacles do look pretty darned insurmountable at first. Before the first time man landed on the moon, it had been impossible up to that point. Changing the impossible into the possible always involves overcoming the obstacles between those two points.

German physicist Albert Einstein, noted for his great accomplishments, once said: "It's not that I'm so smart. It's just that I stay with solving the problem longer."

Einstein did not quit *before* he found a solution. High achievers have learned to see all problems, or at least more of them, as being solvable. Not everyone comprehends this. Lack of achievement often occurs because a person could not figure out how to achieve. The attitude to achieve is one that believes we are limited only by our own thinking. We quit when we stop believing that we can achieve.

"I can't" involves an underdeveloped sense of self that views the external world as being bigger, more powerful and ultimately in control of outcomes. This leaves that person, the lesser-powered one, at the mercy of the stronger. The "I can't" person thinks, "Why bother? It won't make any difference."

The T-Scale is tipped to one side in this case, but it's in favor of the obstacle, not the person. "I can't," "It can't be done" or any variation must be justified or proved right just as all thinking must be. Supporting data, viewpoints, facts and whatever else people can put their hands on will be used to build their case. Everything that does not support this viewpoint is left out. Thought, time and energy are being spent going in the opposite direction to prove the desired outcome is impossible. We really can justify just about anything in our own minds if we try.

If you've never taken the time to notice before, start noticing now. It's easy to do. Just listen to what other people say. Negative, "I can't" comments will involve the relinquishing of personal responsibility, or the shifting of power off of and away from that person and onto someone or something else. You might hear, "I can't do it *because...*" or "It can't be done *because...*" and this explanation will reveal that person's external placement of power. This power shifting is the always-present counterpart to "I can't" thinking that is an easy giveaway to a sense of self that views oneself as being inferior. You may even want to pay closer attention and listen to what you're really saying.

When people become caught up in the negative aspects of a situation or on dwelling on impossibility, they are not at the same time seeing the power they possess to change that situation. They can't see their power because of where they are choosing to place their focus. Remember, you cannot think "I can" and "I can't" at the same time. Nor can you see yourself lacking power and also see yourself having it at the same time. It's one or the other.

This shifting or relinquishing of power screams out the message, "I see myself as the weaker one at the mercy of the external world!" Oblivious to the sabotage their own thinking is doing to themselves, "I can't" thinkers believe they are held back by the external world. If a person sees himself as a victim in a situation, then he also thinks no one could consider him responsible for the outcome that happens. His logic is simple. He is thinking, "Just explain that something or someone else was in complete charge and that takes me off the hook and everyone should understand this the way that I do."

Thinking that relinquishes one's own power to affect an outcome stops the learning process from taking place. Asking oneself, "What could I learn from this and do differently next time?" goes against "There's nothing I could have done about it, so I'm not responsible" thinking. Altering this story would make the negative thinker's explanation no longer credible, so he sticks with it as a way to prove himself right. The cycle then occurs all over again because nothing was learned.

A good example of this is when a person changes jobs because the boss could never understand that the job demands placed on that person were unrealistic and impossible to meet. Oftentimes, these misunderstandings happen over and over in a person's life. People like this might cite another job that treated them unfairly, another terrible boss, more unrealistic demands, and plenty of "if only they'd treated me better" and "Why always me?" sentiments. I remember a story about a low-performing teacher who eventually was released from his job. He responded by saying, "I could have been a better teacher if only I'd had better students."

How we view a specific situation may not be in our own best interest. Changing how you see it may actually do more for you than doing anything else. The tremendous damage of shifting control to an external source is that it belittles the one shifting the control and conceals that person's power, resulting in a continued weakening of his or her self worth.

In essence, we are the ones damaging ourselves. There may be some temporary relief offered in taking responsibility off of oneself for the moment, but the long-term damage to "self" often goes unrecognized because the blame is placed elsewhere. As long as we are steadfast in our thinking and refuse to see any other perspective, our thinking will remain limited.

## ▼ PLAYING BY THE RULES ▼

To think that some or all of our actions do not have any effect or are without consequence is quite simply a misconception and not logical, to say the least. Our participation, effort and persistence, or lack of them, always have an effect of some kind. This is just how it is.

Achievement involves knowing the rules, not ignoring them. In his 1994 book *I Can't Accept Not Trying: Michael Jordan on the Pursuit of Excellence,* professional basketball phenomenon Michael Jordan wrote the following:

**If you're trying to achieve, there will be roadblocks.**
**I've had them; everybody has had them.**
**But obstacles don't have to stop you.**
**If you run into a wall, don't turn around and give up.**
**Figure out how to climb it, go through it, or work around it.**

I don't believe great accomplishment has ever been about achieving only when it's easy and obstacle-free — no way has it ever been about that. And neither has it ever been about having accomplishments freely handed to you without you first doing the necessary work.

Vidal Sassoon, a British hairstylist who built an empire that today includes one of the world's most prominent product lines, is famous for the quote, "Only in the dictionary does success come before work." Success is not about "gimmes" or entitlement, and it isn't handed out merely for good behavior.

Mixing chemicals together will cause a reaction. The reaction is neither right nor wrong, it's just an effect or a result. This is the law of cause and effect. To get a specific chemical reaction as an outcome, you must figure the right formula to mix that will produce that outcome. Every mixture that creates an undesirable reaction is a learning opportunity. It informs you what doesn't work to create the results you want. Your job is to keep trying until you find the right formula to create the outcome you want. This is within your power.

Some people place so much focus on failing that they don't try to succeed. Failure isn't something that should be feared. It doesn't actually occur until a person quits trying — it's merely success in progress up to that point. So when you think about it, you're really in charge of your own success, just don't quit before you find a way to succeed.

These are the rules you must play by when it comes to achievement. So what do you want, special treatment? Do you want to play by a different set of rules than everyone else? Do you think you should be privileged and be allowed to choose which hurdles you want to conquer and those you want to skip? Do you think you should be exempt from disappointing results or from those fabulous obstacle-hurdling learning opportunities that we sometime hate but that actually prepare us for our greatness? Do you want to skip some or all of those opportunities that prove to yourself and everyone else that you really can achieve? Do you want to play by special rules just because you actually see opportunities as difficulties and see projects as being insurmountable problems? Zig Ziglar, a world-renowned motivational speaker and author, once said, "What you get by achieving your goals is not as important as what you become by achieving your goals."

You're not serious when you say you'd like to detour around these wonderful experiences, head straight for the goal and accomplish the same results as those people who actually conquered their challenges and mastered their opportunities, are you? That's not logical. And it's definitely ineffective thinking. You can't expect to mix just any chemicals and have the chemicals alter their normal reaction to fit your desires rather than figure out the right chemicals to mix to get your desired outcome.

You have the prerogative to choose how you use your power. Just realize that what's stopping you, slowing you down, holding you back or even taking your success away may not be what or who you think it is. There can be only one person who determines what you do and what you achieve, and that's you! It's you and your own thinking! If you haven't achieved the desired outcome yet, it's because *you* haven't figured out how. Keep working on it!

These lyrics are in the 1970s Eagles song "Already Gone": *So oftentimes it happens that we live our lives in chains and we never even know we have the key.* These words are about freeing ourselves from the self-imposed bondage of ineffective thought. The key to removing our own shackles is to change the very thinking that sees us shackled and limited in the first place. Our thinking must expose what we're truly capable of, our greatness, and stop deceiving us into believing we are less than we actually are and capable of achieving less than we actually can. Do you believe you can fly?

## ▼ ADOPTING A NEW HABIT ▼

There is a story about classical artist and sculptor Michelangelo, who was asked how he ever created the magnificent lifelike statue of David. If you've ever seen it up close, it looks real enough that it could just walk off its pedestal. Michelangelo responded by saying he had just chipped off the excess rock.

That's what we all need to do. We need to chip away all those unnecessary, ineffective thoughts that contradict our great potential and block the incredible power locked in our minds. Those Kryptonite-like thoughts that drain your power by leading you to believe you can't do something must be shed. What's underneath is magnificent.

When this excess rock is removed, just below the surface is your great potential waiting for the truth to be revealed. Each life is a miracle. No one has ever been created who is irrelevant, inadequate or lacking a potential for greatness.

You are great! You can do it! That's the one-two message you need to learn. You have unlimited potential and can accomplish whatever you make up your mind to do. You just have to learn to believe this for yourself first.

The only difference between a high achiever and someone who achieves less is what this person knows he or she can achieve. What stops a person is "I can't do it" thinking. Just ask a high achiever, and that person will tell you. There really isn't anything that has the power to stop someone who has made up his mind not to be stopped. That message should be becoming loud and clear by now. It's a person's thinking that has the power to both start and stop that person, to keep that person going, to make that person quit. It boils down to this: Change your thinking and change your results.

The key is to harness the power of thought and use it in your favor. It's about being aware of those times when you are not using the power of thought effectively and then switching your thinking over to "How can I?" when you're thinking you can't. Thought is power. If you think, which you do, then you have the power.

Comedienne and entertainer Lucille Ball said: "One of the things I learned the hard way was that it doesn't pay to get discouraged. Making optimism a way of life can restore your faith in yourself."

If you are open to the idea that thinking is a learned process, that there is more than one way to think, and that there could be a more effective way than the one you originally learned, then now happens to be the best time of all to learn more. The toughest part may be giving yourself permission to release your old, ineffective thinking. You're the one who will have to make the commitment to retrain yourself. A new habit can be just around the corner if you give it a chance.

If you haven't made that decision yet, the best thing to do is to put this book down and perhaps pick it up again at a later date. Never feel bad about a decision you've made. You always have the opportunity to change your mind.

There is nothing magical here — no fairly dust to sprinkle or spell to cast that will work in the absence of your effort and commitment to form more effective thinking habits. No one can do this for you, nor can you be made to do this, and there are no shortcuts. Before you can begin, let me tell you that forming a new thinking *habit,* or new autopilot thinking, will be easier when the going is good. The challenge will be when life isn't going so well.

There is a good chance that when you begin switching your well-entrenched thinking that has had operating authority for most of your life, you initially may have contradictory thoughts such as, "Are you nuts? There's no way!" It may even feel absolutely wrong, almost like a lie. That's OK and very normal, especially in the beginning.

Starting a new habit doesn't mean the first time you try it, it's going to instantly take hold. It won't. The old habit must give up some of its ground to make space for the new habit. A lot of times the old will not leave willingly. The incumbent will want to challenge its replacement before it relinquishes its hold.

There's a good chance you won't instantly believe the new thoughts you're thinking are better, but as you begin to see some of the positive results from the power of more effective thought you will begin to believe it more. Then the old, less effective way will more easily surrender. At first it will start out like playing a game, almost as if you are trying to trick your mind. This is how it works. The more you reframe your thinking, the more it will become a conditioned habit.

Changing your mind is really something you've been doing all your life, and it's not as difficult as you may think. You must start somewhere, and this time you'll know the rules better and can be more effective. Your commitment, however, is the most important element of all because you are most likely starting out before you have many successes to lean on and to strengthen you for when tougher times are upon you.

Here's an example: Let's say I have become aware that I'm feeling overwhelmed because I'm being pulled in three different directions on my job. Different areas, which all are very important, are competing for and demanding my time, my budget, my staff and my energy. I have caught myself both thinking and verbally speaking, "I can't do this all. There's no way!" Notice the key phrase "I can't." This is what needs to be eliminated from both my spoken vocabulary and, most importantly, my internal thought process. It must be banished, and "I can do this" needs to replace it — even if I don't believe it at first.

I need to first UN-think "I can't" and then RE-think "I can do this, I just need to figure out a way." As long as I have made up my mind and predicted the outcome as being negative or impossible and am holding onto that, I'm reducing my mental effectiveness and productivity that would lead me to a successful outcome. The very first thing I need to do is switch my thinking over to conceiving the desired outcome as being possible.

Then I need to focus my thought energy into figuring out what it will take to produce this outcome. I need to find a way. I need to switch my limited thinking of "There's no way!" to "Yes I can, so how?" which is thinking that expands until it finds a solution.

It's your choice — constricted thinking or thinking that expands. I will clue you in on a secret. Once you expand your thinking, you'll never want to go back to a limited way of thinking.

Nothing and no one else that comes after this point will do as much to affect your success and determine the outcome than your thinking right here will.

## ▼ RUBBER BAND MAN...OR WOMAN ▼

My job is strictly to provide the message to you and that's it. The rest is solely up to you. My job is to work on my life and your job is to work on yours. In the past, I saw myself as an underdog in several areas in my life, but I no longer do. What changed is that I now have The Attitude.

With that being said, let me share with you a retraining technique that you may want to use that can help you. It helped me. I call it the "Training in a SNAP" strategy. All it requires is you and a rubber band. It will help speed up forming a new habit if you're really committed. Let me tell you from experience, it's especially helpful for when the going gets tough.

Here's what you do. Put a rubber band on your wrist, and every time you catch yourself thinking or saying "I can't" or any variation, SNAP IT just hard enough to feel a little sting. No more than a little pop is needed — it isn't supposed to be negative torture treatment, just a friendly retraining reminder.

That's the UN-think part. Now you must RE-think. Try that same thought again, but this time switch the "I can't" or "It's impossible" with "OK, I know it's possible, I just need to figure out how!" Any variation of "I can, so how can I?" will be satisfactory. Don't laugh. Some people don't even notice, while others know exactly what I'm doing when I'm wearing my fine rubber band jewelry. It can even become be a conversation piece as a way to share *The Attitude*.

Here's another way you can implement this retraining technique. If you are leading a group that needs to brainstorm to come up with a solution to a difficult problem, have each member of the team wear a rubber band during the meeting. Negativity, bad-mouthing, and gripe sessions are stopped quickly with rules understood by everyone that the purpose of the meeting is to work on finding a solution, not on proving it can't be done. Let them do that on their own time if they must. Anyone who gets off track must pay the price of one snap per offense.

For more on the personal side, if you recently got out of a relationship and want to move on but can't seem to stop thinking about the ex, place the rubber band on your wrist and every time you catch yourself thinking about him or her — SNAP IT! Be sure you have two or three replacement thoughts to switch to that do not in any way relate to that person. Think of something positive in your life that's totally unrelated to your ex, perhaps an event in your childhood that makes you smile. To feel better, think happy thoughts.

Every time you make an excuse, shed responsibility, blame someone else, focus on how bad problems are, dwell on negativity, predict doom and gloom, or say "I can't," you're *not* maximizing your power, *you're reducing it.* Being negative is equal to saying "no" to the desired outcome, and it's a byproduct of an untrained, undisciplined mind allowed to run rampant that wreaks havoc on a person's life. Use the rubber band to help you practice and build mental discipline. This is a mental workout that will increase your mental muscle and make you stronger mentally. It will make you more powerful and better equipped to overcome the obstacles you encounter in everyday life.

## ▼ JUST SAY "YES!" ▼

Playwright William Shakespeare said, "It is not in the stars to hold our destiny but in ourselves." We hold the key to our own destiny with the thoughts we think. I remember an event in my life that had a profound impact on me. The quote by Mr. Eden Phillpotts, respected author, poet, and philosopher, "The universe is full of magical things and it's patiently waiting for our wits to grow sharper," sums up my experience.

I was speaking in Phoenix, Arizona, something that I did only about once a year. I had always had the desire to go to the Grand Canyon and see its magnificence for myself, but I had never done it. On this particular trip I kept saying to myself, "Why don't you just go and do it?" I kept coming up with a bunch of reasons why I couldn't or shouldn't. I thought to myself, "I don't have the time. I'd have to change my airline ticket. I didn't pack for a trip to the Grand Canyon. I don't have a rental car. I have no hotel room booked there. I don't want to go by myself." Shall I go on, or do you get my point?

At some point I gave myself permission to say "Yes!" instead of "No!" Suddenly, my thinking aligned with my desires. When I switched my thinking from all the reasons why I couldn't do it to focusing on how I could pull it off, everything seemed to change in that instant — no joke. I made a call to the airline to see whether there were seats open on the same flight on the following day — there were. I called my travel agent and discovered that a hotel within a few blocks of where I was speaking had a car available for rent if I wanted it.

Once I said "Yes!" everything happened so easily, I kid you not. I got a ride to the rental car, got directions and was quickly on my way. When I arrived, I started talking with people in a tour group at the Grand Canyon and they invited me to join them for dinner. I said "Yes, thank you." I ate rattlesnake, which was quite a new experience. Even though I was unprepared for a 50-degree temperature drop that evening, I was generously loaned a sweater to keep me warm. It didn't stop there. I found a beautiful hotel that had room for me, and I saw the most magnificent sunset and sunrise overlooking the Grand Canyon.

My 24-hour extended trip to the Grand Canyon could not have been any more fabulous. And to think, I could have missed this great experience that I had always wanted to do simply by focusing my thoughts on all the reasons why I couldn't. I would have missed the opportunity. How many others have I missed?

It almost makes you want to question whose side I was on originally when I was looking for all the reasons to hold myself back instead of all the reasons to go.

Don't be afraid to find a way. The only thing I have to warn you about is when you start thinking more in *how can I* terms…watch out, because a new world will open up to you. When you discover that you really can, the question then becomes "Do I really want to?"

If you ever want to see the spectacular photographs I took from a disposable panoramic camera, I'll be happy to show them to you. There's this one I have framed. It's a photo with me in it that a fellow tourist was nice enough to take, and on it I have the caption "Just say YES!"

This experience made me aware that I wasn't saying "Yes I can!" in other areas in my life. Perhaps that's the reason I was having so much difficulty achieving the results I desired in those areas. I was using the power of thought to work against myself. I was really getting the equivalent results to the thoughts I was thinking — and just never realized it.

My trip to the Grand Canyon also taught me that you don't have to have all the answers on how to pull something off first, that you can still say "yes" and then figure out how to do it. That's completely OK. In fact, that's exactly how high achievers operate. You don't have to have all the answers before you believe you can. I think we may commonly make this mistake. If we don't know how first, if we're unable to see how it could all come together or if we don't have all the answers, then we think we must say "No." But we don't have to.

Give yourself permission to expand your thinking until you find an option that moves you closer to reaching all your dreams, desires and goals. But you have to say "yes" first. Become aware of how your own thinking is holding you back from achieving what it is you'd like to do. *Awareness is the key.* It is necessary to realize where your thinking has become distorted and is masking the truth, making "I cant's" appear as truths. This thinking is unproductive, ineffective and without benefit — and it's simply not true. It just makes life more difficult for the one who thinks these thoughts.

## ▼ "YES, I CAN!" ▼

The two simple words "I" and "can," combined, can create the most powerful thinking that exists. They can also be separated into two individual fundamental principles. Each of these words has its own unique power, but these words are not nearly as strong apart as they are when they join forces. When they merge, they have the power to change the impossible into the possible.

The "I" portion of this dynamic duo is very important. It's your sense of self, which is how much you recognize your own power. "Can" is the thinking that recognizes truth. Combined, a strong sense of self that thinks "I can" thoughts can conquer those pesky little obstacles that temporarily block the path to achievement. Now add the "YES" onto the front and you've just given yourself an optimistic go-ahead. That's powerful.

American author and lecturer Robert Elias Najemy said: "We alone create our reality. Our power to manifest our preferred reality lies in transforming our beliefs and expectations."

We must transform our thoughts by eliminating all, both in spoken form and thought form, which denies or contradicts the truth about what we really could accomplish if we only believed. Look what we're doing to ourselves. We're shortchanging our potential and holding ourselves back from soaring to great heights simply by the thoughts we are choosing. We are allowing ineffective thinking to bridle our determination to achieve. No one is doing anything worse to us than what we are doing to ourselves.

Now would be a good time for you to question yourself so you can become more aware of your thoughts and the placement of your power.

**What thoughts am I proving right?**

**What outcome am I helping to create on my job? In my personal life? In my relationships?**

**Am I focusing too much on the problem and not enough on finding a solution?**

**Where am I saying "I can't" or "It's impossible," thereby limiting my options, choices and solutions?**

**Do I hold false beliefs about myself and my power to solve my problems? Have I given my power away to someone or something that I falsely think has more power than I do? Do I ever think I'm a victim or that someone or something has control over my life?**

**Can I change my thinking to align more with my goals by thinking thoughts that lead in the direction in which I want to go instead of away?**

Learning to align your thoughts with your desired outcome instead of focusing on all those reasons why something will never happen is the key to achievement. It is what *The Attitude* is all about. You can discover for yourself that you will get further when you shift the focus of your thoughts to follow the directions of your desires. This is called *leading*. Get rid of all the reasons why you can't, or why it won't work. Throw those thoughts out. Let go of them. They're not helping your cause, they're undermining it. *Leading* means to move or to lead yourself in your preferred direction by focusing on thoughts that synchronize with that direction.

Here's an analogy: You are at Point A but you want to be at Point B. Point B is your desired outcome. It is where you want to be or what you want to achieve, and you're not there yet. You have to figure out how to go about accomplishing it, and you have to overcome the obstacles that block your path. You have to think about how to reach the goal, not think thoughts that prevent you from getting there.

If you were going to swim across the English Channel, which would help you the most to reach your goal: to swim with the current or against it? If your desire is to make it to the other shoreline, then this difficult challenge would best be achieved by swimming in the same direction as the current.

"I can" thinking is thinking that is heading in the exact same direction as where you want to go. But here's the problem: We've never realized before that negative thinking takes us in the direction opposite from where we would like to go. We desire to reach Point B, but we go about it by thinking we can't. Our desires say, "Yes I'd like do that, have that or achieve those results" but our thinking regarding attainability says, "but I can't," and then we wonder why all too often we never get where we want to go. But we don't wonder for very long because we just blame our lack of results on something out of our control and continue going about it the exact same way because we didn't learn anything.

It really only makes sense that you achieve more by aligning your thoughts with your desires and not against them. I remember many years ago when I was a staffing manager and I was asked to reduce my next year's budget by 20 percent. I'll be perfectly frank: I thought the idea was absolutely absurd, and let me tell you why.

First of all, this retail organization was growing and planning to open quite a few new stores in the coming year. This meant an increase in hiring, not a decrease. To make it even more difficult, the unemployment rate was falling, which meant there were fewer people in the job market looking for work, and that would make it tougher to fill the new positions. But that wasn't all. With all the changes going on in the company, the turnover rate was up. This meant even more jobs to fill than the year before. How in the world could someone expect the recruiting budget to be cut? It needed to be increased!

It would be really easy to just say, "No way, it can't be done." But the truth was, there was a way to do it, we just had to figure out what that way was. At the very least, if I went back to senior management and declared it to be impossible to do, I'd better be prepared to back up my claim with everything that I had tried first to make this determination. Otherwise, what case would I have?

Believe it or not, once our department sat down with the intention of finding a way, everyone came up with ideas that would allow us to still meet all of our staffing requirements but do it more cost effectively so we didn't go over budget.

Once we started looking, we discovered that one of our most successful sources for hiring was actually one of our least expensive. We also realized that we had become dependent on some very expensive sources for hiring when we really didn't have to be. It wasn't nearly as difficult to accomplish as we first thought it would be, once we put our minds to doing it. In fact, we were quite proud of our accomplishment of doing more with less.

You've got to watch your thoughts constantly, because they can be tricky little devils. When it comes to achieving your desires and goals, you've got to watch yourself to see whether you are thinking constructive thoughts or supporting destructive ones. We think ourselves right out of power by mentally removing our power from ourselves, but we can think ourselves right back into power just as quickly. We can stop the bad habit we learned and replace it with a more effective one at any time.

It's so important to realize what you are actually spending most of your time thinking about, and it might not be what you think it is. Awareness is the first step to changing your thinking. That's when you can quit swimming in the least effective direction, the one that only exhausts people more quickly and produces less-desired results, and then take charge of managing your mind. You cannot rise higher than your own expectations. What are you expecting — that you can't, convinced it'll never happen for you, or complaining that you're just not lucky enough?

If you didn't hear the music before, here again are the lyrics to the Eagles song "Already Gone": *So oftentimes it happens that we live our lives in chains and we never even know we have the key.*

It really is about freeing ourselves from the self-imposed bondage of our own ineffective thought. It's realizing that you hold the key simply by changing what you choose to think about. And you know this choice is yours. It's not any more complicated than that. It's about discovering and unleashing your great potential.

## ▼ IT'S VERY POWERFUL — NOT PRETEND! ▼

There's a saying, "Get knocked down seven times, get back up eight." It's not about denying that you got knocked down or pretending you didn't. Getting knocked down does feel bad. It's an undesirable experience for anyone. But it's about getting back up, dusting off and focusing on moving forward, not about keeping your focus on the fact you got knocked down in the first place and how unfair it was.

Some people have the opinion that "I can" thinking is Pollyanna, or blindly optimistic. It's not really. Once you grasp the true power of thought, you won't consider seeing the bright side as being irrational. It's not about putting on a happy face and pretending the obstacles or projects ahead of you don't exist or won't be a challenge. Positive, "I can" thinking is about recognizing the power you possess to determine the desired outcome and then reaching it by conquering the obstacles in between. It's about expanding your mind until you come up with a solution. It's about thinking that solves problems and engages action, effort and persistence, all of which are ingredients of achievement. It's knowing that you can. And that's not Pollyanna, it's powerful!

Here's another misconception you commonly hear: "I'm just being more realistic than you when I say it'll never work."

It really isn't being more realistic — it's being more fatalistic. It's a false notion that uses the exact same power to sabotage desired results by predicting it can't happen as the "I can" thinking uses to prevail by predicting that it can happen. Thought either aligns with the desired outcome or it does not. "I can" thinking produces more results than "I can't" thinking does, thus making "I can't" thinking not so realistic after all. The word "realistic" is oftentimes used just to package negativity in a way that comes across as more acceptable.

Allowing yourself to believe is the key! Helen Keller did. As someone who had to overcome the obstacles of blindness as a child, and grew up to be a symbol of inspiration, she said, "No pessimist ever discovered the secrets of the stars or sailed to an uncharted land, or opened a new heaven to the human spirit." To discover the secret to the stars for yourself, you must choose to switch from a pessimistic viewpoint to one that is more hopeful that a good outcome is plausible.

It's your call. Changing your thinking is something you must commit to do without requiring anyone else to change first. I know people who would love to hand this book off to someone else that they know could use it and completely miss their own need for it. This is your project without regard to what the outer world does or does not do.

Sometimes we can be like that poorly performing teacher who thinks he needs better students in order to be a better teacher. We want to keep ourselves exactly the same and want the outer world to change to fit our needs and to fill our goals. We make it someone else's responsibility to acknowledge and develop the greatness locked inside ourselves.

We can easily get caught up in flawed thinking that views our desired outcome as being feasible *only* if the external world cooperates by making the necessary changes to produce different results for us. If we don't see these particular changes occurring, then we don't see our desired outcome as being possible. We become dependent on the external world for making or breaking our success and for creating our outcomes.

A simple shift in thinking could make all the difference in the world. It won't actually change the picture or the situation we are in, but by altering our prediction of the impact we imagine our participation will have, from a pessimistic viewpoint to an optimistic one, we will also alter the options that we see available to us.

It's amazing how our thinking instantly expands when we switch it so we can see our power rather than deny it. Possible solutions become apparent where they weren't before. More options mean a larger choice of responses. And when you change your response, you affect the outcome, just as you alter a chemical reaction by changing the chemical combination you mix. It's like a domino effect that is put into motion from a simple shift in your point of view.

The responsibility for our results doesn't belong out there somewhere, nor should it be dependent on the external world. The responsibility is ours and ours alone. If you don't like the results you're getting, change *your* thinking. If you see the external world as having control over your success, then you need to think again. We are not off the hook just because we reject the truth about our own power.

So often, we allow our own potential to be reduced while we misplace our focus on what's wrong all around us. Ghandi said it best: "We must be the change that we wish to see in the world." Shifting your focus and energy onto what you can do better to cultivate your own greatness may be time better spent.

Perhaps a good rule to follow is to only constructively complain about something outside of ourselves when it's followed with a solution *and* backed with the personal action needed to make a difference. Start with yourself. Never just speak idle words and leave a problem for someone else to fix, and never say there is nothing you can do about it. Either contribute to the solution or shift your focus to something more constructive.

## ▼ SEEING EVERYONE'S POWER ▼

We know that some people believe the external world holds all or most of the cards in determining what happens in their lives. These people's locus of control is predominantly external. They see an obstacle as having the greater power, which means it can legitimately and justifiably block not only their success but also everyone else's who encounters them.

They see themselves, as well as most other people, as being powerless to do anything about these success-stealers, and that's just a fact of life. It's only logical to them, then, that anyone who does achieve success did so because that person didn't have the same insurmountable obstacles to block the way. So all they have to do is explain what stopped them, why it was out of their control, and most people should understand, right? They believe that should take them off the hook for the lack of achievement. But it doesn't because not everyone's perception of control is external.

The gap that exists between an internal and an external perception of control is a difference in opinion regarding how much control or power a person has to achieve results by conquering the obstacles that almost always exist. For those people who can see their power, they don't just see it for themselves — they also see everyone else's power. They have learned to see the truth. They see both the hardships that they encounter and those that everyone else encounters as *all* being possible to successfully conquer. They see the power and control that everyone has to have an impact on their own lives, without exception. They see the truth for everyone even if all people don't see the truth for themselves.

So how do you reach those people who need the outside world to understand how insurmountable their hardships are? Those who make excuses for why they can't and believe it themselves? How do you reach people who don't realize they are underestimating themselves and don't understand that the only way their sense of self can be satiated and their greatness acknowledged is via themselves? How do we reach those people who don't know that they actually can achieve their desired results? Or get them to realize that all obstacles can be conquered, or that their thinking might be the biggest obstacle they face and they must face this first? How do you reach those people who think it's everyone else who doesn't understand them when in fact it's they who don't understand? We've got the magic questions figured out, haven't we?

Attitude is about knowing your greatness even if no one else does. It's about realizing that the world outside of you cannot provide you with what you do not provide for yourself. Prosperity is fabulous, and so are all the perks and toys that can come along with it. There is nothing wrong with external gratification — however, it is not a substitute. Recognizing our fullest potential is an inside job, not something that can ever be externally satisfied.

Blaming someone else for your thoughts, for making you feel or behave a particular way, or for what you choose to do or not do is an attempt to assign your authority and power away to the external world. But it doesn't work because this authority cannot be reassigned. This reassignment is only an illusion that appears real to the one thinking it.

We all have our hands full being responsible for ourselves without having to be responsible for someone else, too. As long as people hold onto the false belief that they are powerless, hold onto the illusion that someone or something has control over them, and until their locus of control shifts from external to internal, they will think and act like they're only along for the ride.

●

## ▼ CHANGE YOUR THINKING ▼

Do you realize that when your focus is on the problem and what is so bad about it, you are holding yourself there, in the problem, longer? Focusing on a problem does not lead to a solution. Understand the difference. Dwelling on a problem is dwelling on the problem. If I happen to be somewhat obsessive about how undesirable a situation is, do you know what is not going on? The answer is I'm not thinking about how I can move myself to a more desirable place.

For example, if I'm sick with a cold, I can focus my thoughts on how bad I feel or on what I could do to feel better. If I am quick to believe there is nothing I can do to feel better, I won't put on my thinking cap and engage myself in finding a solution to reach my desired outcome. No action will follow.

Solutions will remain hidden from my view and stay undiscovered as long as I choose to focus on the problem rather than focusing on finding a solution. Your thinking must shift out of the problem into the exploration of every nook and cranny for possible solutions. It's a subtle change in thinking that produces dramatically different results.

Are you familiar with the 1970s song by Paul Simon "50 Ways to Leave Your Lover"? The lyrics read: *The problem is all inside your head, she said to me. The answer is easy if you take it logically. I'd like to help you in your struggle to be free. There must be 50 ways to leave your lover.* The song may take a comical way to make a point, but it explains that we have many options available to us that we quite often can't see or just don't want to see. We just see ourselves as stuck.

We don't always see the light because we're not looking for it. Being problem-focused can let solutions and resolutions slip by undetected because our focus is placed elsewhere. Just as in the song, someone can throw a viable solution in your face or it can just land in your lap and you may not accept it as being possible because you're not in that mindset. I realize that not all ideas and suggestions are valid solutions, but since we don't allow ourselves to be proved wrong too easily, we can shoot down bona fide options without even realizing that's what we're doing. After all, when you're coming from the thinking that has already predicted something's impossible to do, you can easily be blind to how a solution *could* work.

A woman I knew shared with me that she really didn't like the type of work she was doing. I asked her why she didn't do something about it. She responded by telling me there was nothing she could do and continued to explain why this was so. She told me she had no other job skills so she really wasn't qualified to do anything else. She said her age was a disadvantage that was working against her and she couldn't afford to take a cut in pay. She also thought that since the economy wasn't doing so well, another job would be impossible to come by.

This woman had quite a bit of ammunition on her side to prove why she could do nothing to change her situation, and it all sounded legitimate on the surface. But the biggest thing she had going against her was something she hadn't even mentioned or maybe didn't even realize. Her own thinking was her biggest enemy.

I knew this woman personally and knew she was very dedicated and dependable. Her age in no way was going to be an obstacle to prevent her from changing jobs and finding a different employer. That was in her head. She would have been a great hire for anyone, and in the right job she would have been a good employee to invest in with training.

I happened to also know she was eligible to take college classes at no expense to her, allowing her to learn new job skills. She even had a flexible work schedule that would allow her to take classes — another obstacle hurdled. She could pick particular courses that interested her and would align with jobs that would pay her more money than she was currently making.

Regarding her last obstacle, even in a sluggish economy there are still jobs available. They may not be as abundant or as easy to find as they are in a booming economy, but there are still employers needing to fill job openings. Don't forget, she needed some time to take those classes to be prepared for a job change, and in the meantime the economy could improve. She more or less knew this, too. She had talked about doing it but had not followed through because she had already made up her mind.

What she really didn't have going in her favor, the real obstacle that she had to conquer, was her pessimistic thinking. She thought I was being unrealistic.

Without an attitude change here, very little else had much of a chance. How many solutions are you going to come up with when you've already made the determination that there aren't any? Whatever you spend most of your time focusing on — more of the problem or more of the solution — that's what you get more of. It's up to you where your thinking will lead you next.

## ▼ TAKING FLIGHT ▼

Do you realize that it is possible to read to this point, agree with everything written and still not entirely grasp the concept yet? Bear with me, please. I'm not trying to suggest you're stupid — to the contrary, in fact. What I'd like you to do is allow yourself to be open to the possibility that there is still a light bulb moment yet to come. You can be a very smart person filled with a lifetime of lessons and experiences and still not have explored this next point yet.

In the 1939 movie classic *The Wizard of Oz*, the young girl Dorothy who lives on a farm in Kansas is bumped on the head during a tornado, touching off her adventure into the Land of Oz. She meets a scarecrow who wishes he had a brain, a tin man who would love a heart, and a cowardly lion who more than anything wants courage. The entire story is about the obstacles Dorothy and her newfound friends face on their journey to find the Great Wizard of Oz, the only one who can fulfill their desires.

Toward the end of the film, when the Wizard is granting them their wishes, he says to the Cowardly Lion: "As for you, my fine friend, you are a victim of disorganized think-ing. You are under the delusion that simply because you run away from danger, you have no courage. You are confusing courage with wisdom!" When he receives his medal of honor engraved with the word "courage," the Lion replies, "Ain't it the truth! Ain't it the truth!" The only thing that changed when the Lion transformed from cowardly to courageous was his thinking and really nothing else. This change of thinking happened in an instant.

But that wasn't the most profound part of the movie, and neither was the fact that Dorothy and her friends overcame all the obstacles they encountered along the way no matter how big, bad and scary they appeared to be. I believe the best part was when the Wizard was about to leave the Land of Oz to take Dorothy back home to Kansas. Just when his balloon is lifting up, Dorothy's beloved dog, Toto, jumps from her arms. She can't leave without him, so she leaps out of the balloon's basket to retrieve him and it launches without her.

Almost out of the blue, Glenda the Good Witch of the North appears. Dorothy begs for her help. The beautiful witch responds, "You don't need to be helped any longer. You've always had the power (to go back to Kansas)." Confused, Dorothy responds, "I have?" Even the Scarecrow jumps in and asks, "Then why didn't you tell her before?"

Here is the part that is so hard to believe was written so many decades ago and was so profoundly ahead of its time. The Good Witch answers, "Because she wouldn't have believed me. She had to learn it for herself!" Dorothy is asked what she has learned and responds, "Well, I think that it wasn't enough to just want to see Uncle Henry and Auntie Em."

Unfortunately, I think there are many who haven't yet learned how to use the power of thought effectively because they just don't believe it yet for themselves deep down inside. That's why we look outside of ourselves for an external Wizard to grant us our dreams, goals and desires by removing the obstacles that block our path — all because we don't believe we can do it for ourselves. If you haven't seen *The Wizard of Oz* lately, it's a lot of fun to watch it for its deeper message.

I think there are still many who don't comprehend that it's not enough to have dreams or just to want to reach a goal. The simple truth is that the power to convert desires into reality belongs to each individual, and it's up to each person to make this happen. The Scarecrow with his brains says, "But it's so easy, I should have thought of it for you, Dorothy." "No," the Good Witch says, "she had to find it out for herself."

And you, too, must discover for yourself the power that's within you. Until you do, until you change your thinking about this, not only will you simply not believe, you will produce fewer results than you could.

You may be a person who understands this intellectually. A lot of people do. But not all people who know this apply it to their own lives or even know exactly how. Comprehending the power of thought and applying effective thinking everywhere in your life can be a bigger project than you may realize at first. I find the comprehension of this is something that occurs in degrees or stages and isn't something that comes packaged in knowing it all or knowing nothing. If it were, then most people probably would declare that they already fully and completely understand it all and have nothing else to learn and nothing new that they can apply to their own lives. Isn't it absolutely amazing what we can believe if we want to. Closed-mindedness is equivalent to constricted thinking.

## ▼ SEEING THE OPPORTUNITY ▼

If you don't see the opportunity that's in front of you, how can you say "Yes, I can"? You can't seize it if you can't see it. I remember a difficult time I was going through. I had trouble seeing the opportunity that existed. It was a time when several people in my life who meant a lot to me suddenly moved on and left a tremendous void in my life.

I knew that the angle in which I chose to see this situation and where I placed my focus would make all the difference in the world in getting through this tough time. I was mentally disciplined enough in my thinking to focus my thoughts on the fact that there was good that would emerge from this even if I didn't know what it was at the time — and I didn't. My positive attitude focused on the bright side instead of on the darkness that would have kept me wallowing in misery for an extended period of time.

But I have to be truthful: I was floundering. It was a sad place and I didn't like being there.

To ease the pain I was feeling, I kept my focus on the good times I had shared with each of these people. But still sometimes I would think about how much it hurt when I was missing them. When I caught myself thinking about how much I had lost, I would switch my thinking over to having faith that there had to be good just around the corner. When

I was feeling sad, I would switch my thinking over to one of my many happy memories and quickly found myself smiling while appreciating the opportunity to have had these people in my life. All this thinking was fine, but it only offered temporary relief. It was helping me to feel less pain or sadness at the present moment, but it wasn't doing anything to move me forward to a better place. Positive as I was, without seeing the opportunity that existed here, being positive was getting it only halfway right.

Think of it this way. I was at Point A, which is always where you are in the present moment. As disciplined and even as helpful as they were, my positive thoughts alone were keeping me stuck at Point A. It's almost as if my own thinking was holding me back from moving forward to a more desirable destination because I wasn't thinking about that yet. My thoughts were not *leading* me to any other place. Sure, I'd eventually get tired of being here and would automatically move on in my thinking. However, that could take some time. If I wanted to, I could help this process along just by putting some deliberate thought into it.

A more desirable destination for myself, also referred to as Point B, could be whatever I envisioned it to be. It's similar to the beginning of the book where we talk about how we unconsciously predict what is likely to happen and act accordingly, except this time it's about consciously choosing the particular outcome that you want to have happen or the specific results that you want to achieve. It's about focusing on those thoughts that support this outcome as being possible and from there automatically acting accordingly to prove this thinking right. We're not going to "do" effectively or "be" effective until we think effectively. That's how you can tell when your thinking is optimal, because it's the genuine optimistic thinking that produces action. If the action is missing, check the thinking.

Realize that Point B is an ever-present opportunity that is only limited by our imagination. By "opportunity," I mean the chance to see the power we have to turn our wishes into reality. The problem is, however, we so often miss seeing the opportunity because we don't see ourselves as having the power to produce any of these outcomes we desire. You could say destiny is what you create for yourself by either choosing or by letting it be chosen for you. Really, both are your choice.

*The Attitude* is not about learning how to achieve, because you already are achieving. It's about learning how to produce more of the desired outcomes that you want to achieve. Focusing on the positive while hoping for the best to happen is not thinking that acknowledges the power we have to create the "what comes next" part.

For the longest time I was only "getting" the power of thought intellectually — I was not applying it to my life. I had help from a close friend, author Maxine Jones, who encouraged me to look at my situation from a different viewpoint. She helped me to see the opportunity and the power that I actually had available to use all along but didn't quite realize.

Here's the advice she gave me: She said to look at this extra space in my life as if I had just cleaned out a closet. You don't need to label this experience as being either good or bad, she told me, because the extra space is neither, it just *is*. If you need to label it, call it an opportunity, one to create something new or better in your life. Think of it as a blank canvas on which you can paint anything you want. It is limited only by your imagination.

Have you realized lately for yourself the opportunities that are available to you right now to create more of what you want in your own life? If you don't believe you can achieve, then you cannot see these opportunities. They are there. They are just hidden from your view because of your different viewpoint. Think about my scenario. When I was feeling powerless, I thought all I could possibly do was sit back and hope my new space would be filled with something I liked, and hopefully soon. You know, keep myself positive and hope for the best outcome. After all, that's all a person can really do, right?

Not very motivating, is it? Now, what if I could *see for myself* that I held the power to determine what would fill this space? It changes the picture, doesn't it, but it does so without changing anything in reality. What comes with seeing your power is also seeing more choices, or more choices that you can see as being actual options.

Think of the unlimited possibilities I had. I could keep this new extra space in my life unfilled if I chose and could use this time for myself to relax. I also had the option to fill this space back up, and it could be with almost anything I wanted it to be. It was totally up to me. I could start an exercise program and begin bike riding, which I had wanted to do for a while. I could become more active in my volunteer work. I could focus on making new friends or on attending social events that interested me. I could spend more time working so I could get caught up on projects. I could start a hobby, take a class. Get my point?

All of this was under my control. What's important to realize is that I had an opportunity to create what I wanted, if I wanted. Opting not to do anything with this opportunity is different than not seeing I had an opportunity. Before, I wasn't even realizing that I had one. I was just trying to figure out how to feel less sad and was switching my thoughts over to happier times in the past, which was *leading* nowhere new.

My thinking before was what was preventing me from seeing the opportunity that was there all along. I finally could see how I was limiting myself and even preventing myself from taking flight. I wasn't doing anything to help myself move from a place that I found undesirable to someplace preferable. All of a sudden I could see what I couldn't see before. Nothing changed except my thinking.

Now I was feeling motivated and empowered. I had to think about what outcome or results I really wanted, what was my Point B, the desired destination. Before you can begin painting the canvas, you have to have a picture in mind. That will guide you to pick the right colors and brush strokes to create that image. Painting is not something you do when you have no picture in mind or you don't see your power to create.

Just selecting or envisioning the desired outcome isn't enough, however. Most of the time we have no trouble with the part about making wishes. What we have the tendency to do is make the wish and then stop there. What comes next is most important.

Once the goal is set, there needs to be the right type of thinking to support it. The goal has to be thought of as being possible. It has to be envisioned, and don't take for granted that's something we always do. I had to align my thinking with the destination I had chosen. I had to think, "I can achieve this — now let's figure out a way how!" I had to think about how I could accomplish this, and not about how it would never be available to me.

I'd like to say we can't skip the step of aligning our thoughts with our destination, but it's something we do all the time, unfortunately. We go about trying to achieve a certain outcome via the route of thinking that we can't or by thinking we lack opportunity. We express our desires and that's it. We think about other things.

Ever notice that when you think clashing thoughts about achieving your desires, you don't get very far? Now you know why. We shoot ourselves down before we even take flight because of the specific type of thoughts, pessimistic ones, which we choose to think. But it really doesn't have to be that way.

We need to realize that opportunities are ever-present right in front of us. Right now, you are standing in the doorway of unlimited potential. We always possess the power to create. In fact, that's what taking flight and soaring means, to create or achieve. All you have to do is once you have Point B, your desired outcome, clearly in sight, align your thoughts so they lead you in *that* direction. Every time you catch yourself thinking or saying something that is contrary to your desired results, let a SNAP on the wrist with a rubber band be your minor repercussion instead of the consequences that come along with sabotaging thoughts.

SNAP is your cue to UN-think and then to RE-think. If you are caught unprepared without a rubber band, an alternative retraining technique is to mentally (meaning silently) shout the word "STOP!" every time.

To replace an old habit of thinking with new thoughts, you must stay with this long enough to see results. Every time you catch yourself relinquishing your own power to create, every time you think or say "I can't" or "It can't be done," when you make someone or something else responsible for your results, or you choose to give up instead of continuing to try, it's *you* who must elect to change this and select another option. This book is less a step-by-step guide to more effective thinking and more of a wake-up call for *you* to see the light and take flight.

Once that light bulb moment occurs and you can see your own power, you'll make the commitment to yourself. The rest is easy! Until that happens, this information or anything similar, and the source doesn't matter, will seem nonsensical and ridiculous. You will believe this information to be over-simplified, unsympathetic, unrealistic and lacking real-life application. For a person's motivation to truly increase, "I can" thinking must be embodied and integrated more than it had been prior. Otherwise this message can at best offer only a temporary motivational spurt because it remains external and will quickly be forgotten.

You are the one who must recognize your own thinking that endorses any behavior that sabotages your success. Only you can choose to stop the power drain on yourself. Even though it is only in your mind that you are relinquishing your power when you do that, it's in the mind that all our power exists. To think is to have power.

## ▼ PRODUCING EXTRAORDINARY RESULTS ▼

The good news is we are all already halfway there, without having to do anything at all. Our built-in device designed to prove us right is already operational and is ready and waiting for our commands. It takes its orders from our every thought — yes, every thought, not just a selected few. That's how it's been working all along.

The power we possess with more effective thought is exactly the same as the power we've always had. The difference is to consciously harness the power of "I can!" and to use it more to our own advantage, and that's what is making us more effective. The challenge is to begin managing what we think by deliberately choosing productive thoughts rather than allowing them to run without any boundaries.

It's only when you comprehend your power to create that you can take control of the wheel and navigate where you want to go. A person can't help but see himself as merely a passenger in life instead of the captain of his own ship otherwise. As a passenger, you can only wish and wait for what comes next and hope for the best. Even reading this book won't make any difference. It's something that YOU have to buy into and believe for yourself, just as Dorothy learned in *The Wizard of Oz*.

For the longest time, I missed seeing myself in the role of creator, that is creator of my own desired outcomes or empowered producer of results. I now see my life in the mode of constantly creating. I ask, what's my goal and how am I going to get there? In fact, I see a masterpiece in progress. Sam Walton, founder of the Wal-Mart empire, said, "High expectations are the key to everything." Reaching Point B tomorrow, whatever it may be, is completely dependent upon what I think and do today.

What a fabulous idea. Create a life filled with whatever I truly make up my mind to achieve, and what a good life that could be. Just so you know the rest of the story, I no longer have that empty space that I found so undesirable. I envisioned my ideal Point B and then focused on creating exactly that outcome. It was a relatively simple project, and I had fun shaping it along the way, but it's a way to look at all of your life, both personally and professionally.

Frank Maguire, former CEO for Federal Express, said, "The best way to predict your future is to invent it." Achievement is a natural and normal part of life. Unfortunately, however, lessons in how to achieve haven't been quite so routine. We go through life pressured to achieve without necessarily being taught how to do it. Some of us have even been taught the opposite information, to concede our own limitations and to not get our hopes too high.

Do you really think we are achieving all we could with thinking that advocates limited accomplishment? If we are achieving only a portion of what we could and we are thinking effectively only a fraction of the time, do you think there is any connection between the two? Let me ask you, do you now believe that no thought has power, some thought has power, or all of your thoughts have power? Maybe you'd like to believe that only your optimistic thoughts, like a placebo, have power and all other thoughts are inconsequential. I think most people live their lives not taking the full power of thought seriously.

Can you conceive the possibility that *all* thoughts, every one of the 90,000 per day, have equal power? How about what Einstein believed, that high achievers simply produce more results not because they have something special that others don't, but that they are ordinary people who produce extraordinary results because of the way they think and what they believe about achievement? Are you ready to understand that all of us can unleash our own power that's locked within?

## ▼ HAVE THE ATTITUDE THAT HIGH ACHIEVERS HAVE! ▼

W hether it's a project or goal that your employer has set for you such as a sales quota, or one you personally want to achieve, that doesn't matter. Whether it's a health problem that you'd like to heal or a relationship that you'd like to mend, it's your commitment that is paramount. To realize that ineffective thinking is shortchanging our own potential to achieve the outcome that we want can be quite empowering by itself. But understanding that we have the power to change our thinking at any time may perhaps be our greatest revelation of all. Clement Stone, a captain of industry who grew up during the Depression reading Horatio Alger novels and went on to write about success through a positive attitude, said, "There is one thing over which each person has absolute inherent control and that is control over their mental attitude."

When we become convinced of a certain outcome, we act accordingly to prove our thinking right. We can't help but do just that because that's how we're wired. But what we can help, what we do have control over, is what thoughts we choose to think. We can get into the habit of positively believing that something can be achieved, that we can do it, especially in those places where we didn't think we could.

U.S. first lady Eleanor Roosevelt once said, "You must do the things that you thought you couldn't do." Imagine what you could achieve with a mind full of "I can" thought energy instead of focusing on "It can't be done." We can consciously change our thinking to thoughts that *lead* in the same direction that we want to go in, instead of responding haphazardly out of old habit, in a direction that sabotages our desired results. The more you believe and the more you focus on "I can do it," the greater the energy you give to shaping that outcome and making it a reality.

Optimism or "I can" thinking is just a learned habit, no more and no less. So is pessimism. You can keep your negative viewpoint that you learned before you knew any better — no one is going to take it away from you. However, I can tell you that if you desire to achieve more, like high achievers do, you'll get further ahead with *The Attitude* than you will without it.

Sporadically engaging in effective thought will produce only sporadic results. In fact, we're *all* already doing it on an inconsistent basis, but some people are doing it more part-time than others. Jumping back and forth between optimism and pessimism or between "I can" and "I can't" thinking can wreak havoc on the results a person achieves. Thinking effectively is not thinking that you can turn off and turn back on and expect optimum results. For it to be *The Attitude*, it must be a habit, a predominant way of thinking that governs your life in order for you to produce the most results.

There is a story about a Native American grandfather who tells his grandson: "Sometimes I feel as if I have two wolves fighting inside of me. One wolf is the negative, vengeful, angry one. The other wolf is the upbeat, kind, optimistic one." The grandson asks him, "Which wolf will win the fight?" The grandfather answers, "The one I feed." So, which one are you feeding?

Every thought counts. Every thought has power. Become obsessed not with negativity, worry and fear, but immersed in thinking that contributes to your success. U.S. President Abraham Lincoln phrased it this way: "Always bear in mind that your own resolution to succeed is more important than any one thing." Adopt this belief for yourself and you will see how effortless it can be to learn to fly high — in fact, there is no other way.

Too many of us for too long have thought that for some reason it's bad to be great. It's not! In fact, it's much worse to not believe you can find solutions and solve problems when you actually *could*. Worse would be to *not* comprehend what you *could* indeed achieve and to allow your achievements to go unaccomplished. And worst of all would be to *not* fathom just how great you really are and the power that you really have available to you and instead to go though life thinking that you are less!

It can be boiled down to what Terry Josephson said: "No matter where you go or what you do, you live your entire life within the confines of your head. Stop thinking in terms of limitations and start thinking in terms of possibilities." Remember, your attitude is not a reflection of your life. Instead, your life is a reflection of your attitude. "I can't" is a block that you can remove that will greatly change and improve your mental vision. If you are ready, now is the best time to make a pact with yourself, a covenant to live by from this point forward, and that is to...*Have The Attitude!* To fly is to achieve. Equipped with *The Attitude,* you can fly high. Let your feet lift from the ground and they'll never touch down as long as you believe.

I'd like to close with a message composed by the inspiring writer and actor David Geiger, who is a personal friend of mine. It's called *Dreamers.*

### Dreamers

One day you wake up, look around and wonder, Where did it all go? What happened to the passion, the dreams and the causes that inspired you in your vision of the future?

We think we will live forever, that time has no bearing on us, because we are that one special individual to which the laws of nature do not apply. We don't accept the fact that we are going to die, that one day the life we know will just end.

We can see the madness of forgotten dreams around us. They said, "I'll do it tomorrow," but they've said it one too many times and now they've run out of time. We will die, time will go on, and our dreams will be taken by another dreamer to follow a procrastinator's path, or to live the dream.

There are so many who have forgotten what it feels like to lose oneself into a passion. Just look in their eyes. They have given up on their destiny. The past is gone. What we can control is what happens next. Will we try again, or will we just give up?

Quitting is easy. It's often the popular choice because anyone can do it. The quitters union does not discriminate — it accepts all.

There's a war going on inside each and every one of us, and our true selves are losing the battle. We think it could never be, so we never try. We have become afraid of the unknown. We've even become comfortable with the misery of forgotten dreams.

Our passion for life is being sucked away, and we are dying on the inside, years before we die on the outside.

But we must not forget what we love, or why we are here. We must remember that little kid who wanted to change the world. We must wake up and do. No one wants to look back and regret his time. Wouldn't it be better to look back and smile?

Follow your heart. That's how we truly defy the laws of nature, and that's how we become great. And that, my friend, is what life is all about, that is why we are here. It takes desire to start the game, it takes courage to play the game, and it takes dedication to finish the game.

It's time to put our fears aside. They've led the way too long. It's time to wake up. It's time to live!

For more information, please visit
The Carol Quinn Organization at
www.CarolQuinn.Org

## Our Philosophy

Many non-profit and community programs provide assistance without permanently advancing individuals toward actualizing their maximum potential. Without a change in a person's learned way of thinking, detrimental behavior continues. Assistance programs can act as a bandage only as long as the cause continues to exist.

To have a long-term effect, aid must be combined with education. Mental limitations, a low sense of self-worth and a belief of powerlessness must be replaced with a new knowledge and understanding focused on personal potential, choice and control. Education must reach individuals in a way that truly allows the replacement of old thoughts with new ones in order for new behaviors to arise and remain. From there, tools and support should be provided as an aid.

**Our organization is dedicated
to these beliefs and principles.**

## About The Author With Attitude

Renowned business author and keynote speaker Carol Quinn is the leading expert in understanding the common thread that all high performers share — The Attitude! In her previous book, *Don't Hire Anyone Without Me! A Revolutionary Approach to Interviewing and Hiring the Best,* Quinn helped employers improve their hiring by teaching them how they could better identify the true high achievers from those pretending to be. Now she puts her knowledge and easy-to-read style to work on a more personal level, moving from *Hiring The Attitude* to *Having The Attitude* in this latest book. Quinn is president and founder of Hire Authority, Inc., a company that specializes in training interviewers. Her cutting-edge methodology involving Motivation-Based Interviewing was derived from her experience in interviewing thousands of applicants in corporate America.

---

### There's Only One Thing Better Than Reading the Book... Experiencing It for Yourself!

#### Share The Attitude!

- Available as a keynote speaker, Carol Quinn is a corporate must!
- Invite us to your workplace for an on-site *Have The Attitude!* workshop.
- Order your *Have The Attitude!* Kit. Great for corporate meetings, contests and incentives. Your company cannot afford to not *Have The Attitude!*

### Call toll-free 1-866-638-0313 for details and pricing

Visit www.HaveTheAttitude.com

**Hire The Attitude!**

As an employer, how can you recognize the real high performers from the imposters? *Don't Hire Anyone Without Me!* is a how-to book that shows you how to incorporate **Motivation-Based Interviewing** into your hiring process.

Learn how to avoid the most common pitfalls of hiring, such as making decisions based on skills alone, or basing a decision on a "gut feeling" about a candidate. Learn how to assess an applicant's Attitude.

Trade paperback, $13.99
ISBN: 1-56414-577-8
Career Press, 2002
189 pages, 5¼" by 8⅛"

• As a keynote speaker, Carol Quinn shares her insight into hiring high performers in any industry.

• Teach all your managers how to identify and hire the best. Call for information about our full-day and half-day workshops on *Hiring The Attitude.*

• Your organization can both *Hire The Attitude* and *Have The Attitude!* Combination packages are available.

**Call toll-free 1-866-638-0313 for details and pricing**

Visit www.HireAuthority.com